Starving in the silences

Starving in the silences

An exploration of anorexia nervosa

MATRA ROBERTSON

NEW YORK UNIVERSITY PRESS
Washington Square, New York

First published in the USA in 1992 by
NEW YORK UNIVERSITY PRESS
Washington Square
New York, N.Y. 10003

Library of Congress Cataloging-in-Publication Data

Robertson, Matra.
    Starving in the silences : an exploration of anorexia nervosa/
Matra Robertson.
        p.   cm.
    Includes bibliographical references and index.
    ISBN 0–8147–7434–2 (cloth)   —ISBN 0–8147–7435–0 (paper)
    1. Anorexia nervosa—Social aspects.   2. Anorexia nervosa—
Psychological aspects.   3. Women—Psychology.   I. Title.
    [DNLM: 1. Anorexia Nervosa.   2. Women—psychology.   WM
175 R663s]
    RC552.A5R63   1992
    616.85′262—dc20
    DNLM/DLC
    for Library of Congress   92–16188
                                                                    CIP

Manufactured in Singapore

Contents

Acknowledgments

I would like to acknowledge and thank Alan Davis for generously commenting on various drafts and for his encouragement, interest and critical support in this project. I particularly thank Peta Tait for her sustained understanding, thoughtful suggestions and patience. I am also grateful to my family, friends and colleagues for their interest over the past years in my writing as an extension of my work with women who have been to the extremes of eating disorders and returned. My hope is that such women will find the courage to write and speak about their experiences and subvert the discourse for themselves.

Preface

The modern age demands that the human body not only be observed, gazed upon, but that it also be assessed. The body—especially the female body—is exhorted to conform to models in the way the soul once was: quite simply, some bodies are divine, objects of worship, thoroughly good and pure, and these are the bodies we must strive for.

Out of this world arises anorexia nervosa, the phenomenon of wastedness which parodies the beautiful female body while attempting to achieve it. As an image or a metaphor for the female's response to the dictates of femininity it is compelling: and it's hardly surprising in this body-scrutinising modern age that anorexia has come under particular scrutiny itself.

But the phenomenon is not a new one. The behaviour of self-starvation has been around for centuries but only began to be called a disease in the eighteenth century with the rise of the medical profession's power.

Anorexia nervosa is therefore a relatively recent label, but it is a phenomenon which appears to be on the increase. The examination of it is certainly on the increase, with a wide range of treatments in and outside the mainstream medical profession. These treatments, however, while perhaps not as violent as they used to be, still cannot claim to be hugely successful.

I am concerned with what the modern world is doing when it turns its discursive gaze on the phenomenon of anorexia nervosa, and how the concept of 'anorexia nervosa' is not conducive to expressing meaning for women who starve themselves.

Introduction

It was my experience of sitting with women diagnosed as anorexic who wanted help and a way out of their immense feelings of hopelessness, despair, loneliness and secrecy that prompted me to write this book. The literature on anorexia nervosa, however, is extensive and crushes impulses to search out different ways of understanding.

Nevertheless, anorexia nervosa—as a 'phenomenon' increasingly experienced by women in Western society—demands attention and demands new ways of understanding it.

I am also interested in how these so-called anorexic women come to be consumers of psychiatric services. A commitment to feminism has informed my practice as a health worker for the past sixteen years in both women's health centres and government community health centres. These services give women from many different backgrounds the opportunity to receive counselling, as voluntary participants, in a non-institutional community setting. My contact with women in different states of emotional health, and the impact of the psychiatric profession on women's lives, have led to my concern about how women come to define themselves as ill and to seek help from therapists and physicians.

The health service that treats women with anorexia nervosa administers treatment on the basis of gender (Ehrenreich & English, 1973; Levy, 1976). The medical profession is basically granted self-regulation by the State, and has established legitimacy as the primary professional group caring for the anorexic. Women working in health services, private therapists, and feminists working in women's health services operate in a set of institutions where doctors still have the greatest professional power. Women who work as counsellors, social workers, psychiatric nurses, psychotherapists and health workers do so in an environment which is still dominated by male normative values. Medical practitioners define their own and others' areas of competence. Therefore, the feminist health worker is less likely to have her forms of practice validated, as male medical dominance is challenged by the existence of feminist practice (George, 1986).

Women who are diagnosed as anorexic and become consumers of the health-care system may find themselves forced to submit to treatment they do not want. Medical practitioners have assumed the moral duty of providing treatment—against the patient's will, if necessary. In September 1988 in Sydney, the case of two young women aged 17 and 19 who were diagnosed as anorexic and were patients in Macquarie Psychiatric Hospital was widely reported in the popular press (*Daily Telegraph*, *Sun-Herald*). The teenagers were made involuntary patients. It was reported that they were scheduled, i.e. detained against their will, for one and three months respectively. During this time they were force-fed, and they attempted, without success, to use legal procedures to avoid this.

Feminists have developed alternative theories of health practice, but have been less successful in establishing their legitimacy as providers of alternative forms of treatment. Feminist health workers can promote change in individual women and draw their attention to the negative effect of oppressive social structures, yet they have had minimal impact on the ideological and political basis of health service organisations. As a feminist working within community mental health services, I have found that the feminist health worker's role is contradictory, as it is often located within an organisation which reinforces the dominant gender order and the legitimacy of members of the medical profession as the dominant care-givers. Some feminists do work in private practice, with a standard fee of between $50 and $80 an hour. This autonomy minimises medical meanings and intrusion in therapeutic work, but only some women can afford such non-refundable therapy fees.

In the dominant gender order, the boundary for women between illness and normality is a fragile one. Gender definitions vary across societies, yet women's oppression everywhere limits the possibilities for them to be self-determining. Women choose from these limited possibilities available to them, possibilities which are further restricted by race, class, education and access to contraception. Becoming a woman involves a transition and shaping of her femininity by culture. Culture regulates the appropriate shape for women.

Patterns of dieting and food consumption among the so-called normal population are problematic, to say the least. Food and diet contain cultural meanings, and there are variations in what food signifies in society. Moreover, food consumption is a result of complex economic, technological and political factors which influence consumption patterns for both men and women. Food consumption, in common with gender prescriptions on eating and embodiment, is a major element in the ideologies of different societies.

It is in this complex context that anorexia nervosa, an extreme form of 'normal' dieting behaviour, emerges. The question of how anorexia nervosa creates meaning for women is one over which medicine and feminism have differed. Simply put, the former has anorexia as a type of psychiatric illness, while the latter most often sees anorexic behaviour as a symptom of women's oppression in a patriarchy. As Lacan and feminist theorists have observed, the unconscious has a major role in mediating our ability to find meaning in the world. Regrettably, Elizabeth Grosz's volume on Lacan was not available for consultation at the time of writing (Grosz, 1990). Anorexia nervosa is simply one of many choices that women can make to express themselves within a dominant gender order where women's power is unequal to men's. The conceptualisation of anorexia nervosa needs to include an analysis of culture in the unconscious.

I have used the term self-starvation at times to contrast with the medical term anorexia nervosa, and in order to describe the behaviour in a manner outside the disease model.

This is not a book which attempts to add to the literature on anorexia nervosa. While I do explore the phenomenon of anorexia, and the medical and feminist responses to it, my aim is broader. It is to shed the layers (as the self-starver sheds layers in search of herself) of a discourse which has created anorexia nervosa and which its sufferers now inhabit.

In the process, two main questions have emerged. First, how does the label anorexia nervosa make the experience of self-starving explicable or meaningful to the starver? I argue that, as a category of illness, anorexia was created because it made meaningful to the medical profession—not the starver—a set of symptoms and patterns of behaviour which were unreasonable and inexplicable. Anorexia nervosa was rendered an abnormality by a discourse which was privileged to define what was normal. This discourse is patriarchal and also medical, and I believe the anorexic patient has little hope of finding herself inside it.

The second question grew out of the first. What does the example of anorexia nervosa tell us about the experience and meaning of femininity in our culture? How does the female create herself within a masculine discourse? It seems to me that language is central here. We inhabit discourses which are not our own, yet may appear to be. In the structure and language of these discourses we try to make sense of the world and ourselves. This attempt may partially succeed, may be full of contradictions, or may fall altogether.

In exploring the construction of the self-in-the-world (in this case, the female self), I have made considerable use of the theories of Foucault and have also used the theories of Lacan, Irigaray and others.

All of them have helped in the effort to shed layers. I hope that in the process light is also shed.

1 Cultural meanings of eating and food

Anorexia nervosa is on the increase in the West, in societies which themselves are increasingly obsessed with food, diet, shape and body image. People are instructed what to eat and how to 'burn it off', they are tantalised with forbidden food, then chided for their failure to resist it. In this chapter, I look at the cultural context of anorexia nervosa, and at the way in which food and eating are loaded with meanings which we ingest, digest and regurgitate. Anorexia arises in a culture that makes eating a problematic conversion of nature by culture.

Food and diet are part of a complex set of meanings in any culture. The production and consumption of food are part of the way in which people come to understand the world. Food and diet contribute to the construction of the individual's sense of self in society:

> consumption decisions become the vital source of the
> culture of the moment. People who are reared in a
> particular culture see it change in their lifetime: new
> words, new ideas, new ways. It evolves and they play a
> part in the change. Consumption is the very arena in
> which culture is fought over and licked into shape.
> (Douglas & Isherwood, 1979:57)

'Normal' behaviour about diet and food is progressively established by lay and medical discourse, and offers subjects of this discourse, i.e. the general population, the choice either of docilely accepting the norm or of deviating from it and thereby coming into the domain of medical

1

treatment. In the production of 'truth' about correct diet and eating habits, medicine exercises power by categorising and labelling the ordinary person's private activity of eating. The ordinary eater interacts with the medical profession in a context disciplined by that profession's 'knowledge' about food quality, adequacy and quantity.

For example, in Sydney in 1990 a 24-hour medical centre took out half-page advertisements in local newspapers telling people to check their 'healthy weight' (i.e. what they felt was healthy and how they looked) against a medical table of desirable weight for height. A $30 a week medically supervised replacement meal program and an exercise program were part of the medical support offered to achieve 'ideal' weight. Readers were advised to 'just come in' to their nearest 24-hour medical centre ('we care 24 hours a day'), and have their Diet Slim program consultation with a medical practitioner. Dieting is a widespread preoccupation among women, who commonly overestimate their weight and believe they are 'too big'. Members of a population of normal weight would perhaps be the prospective customers for this 24-hour medical centre. Preoccupation with weight and fear of weight gain are cited in the literature as common symptoms of anorexia nervosa (Slade & Russell, 1973). Yet the concept of an 'ideal' shape is one that 'normal eaters' share with anorexics.

Culture, food and diet

How food is produced and consumed is influenced by environmental, technological, political and economic factors. Food consumption also reflects the quality of life for people of various status and power positions in stratified societies. Cross-disciplinary studies demonstrate the cultural factors associated with food, diet and eating habits (Montgomery & Bennett, 1979; Shack, 1971). Hunger or appetite is a mental response to physiological deficits, and a motivator of various social activities such as cooking, food-gathering and, in some instances, hunting. Internal cues which are a combination of learnt behaviours, palatability, cultural norms and food availability provide individuals with messages about when and what to eat, and when sufficient food has been consumed. Yet before the eighteenth century taste preference did not determine what the majority of people in Europe ate. Food shortages were the most common determinant of hunger, and people may have desired foods that were simply not available.

In the Judaeo-Christian tradition the Fruit of Knowledge was consumed before sexual activity (sin). This association of food and desire is common in various cultures. The organ which consumes food—the mouth—is an erogenous zone in Western culture, and the eroticisation of the breast in that culture has created a further link between sex and eating (Farb, 1980). In Western society, adjectives such as 'hungry', 'starved', 'satisfied' are used to describe both sex and eating. Women can be described as 'spicy', 'a dish', 'good enough to eat', and men as 'meat', 'a hunk'. Sexuality can be discussed in terms that relate to both food and eating.

Studies such as Anne Murcott's of the philosophies of eating have described culture-based moral attitudes to food and eating. 'Indeed what and how people eat or drink may usefully be understood in terms of a system whose coherence is afforded by the social and cultural organisations with which it is associated' (Murcott, 1984:1). Culture informs the individual about the 'right' food to eat and the 'correct' way in which it is to be eaten. Blaxter and Paterson's (1984) study of 58 families in Scotland showed that 'goodness' in food was a matter not simply of nutritional factors, but also of moral beliefs about the dangers of affluence, in that 'good' food was often cheap and plain food, as opposed to 'rubbish' tinned food, which was generally more expensive.

In the United States today the increase in the consumption of refined sugar as a source of carbohydrates at the expense of complex starches such as grains, vegetables and fruit has led to poor nutrition among some of the population. This is in a society with a grain surplus.

Australian studies show that higher socioeconomic groups eat a more nutritious diet with more fresh fruit and vegetables. The poor, the working class and Aborigines do not have an adequate intake of nutrients, and have a higher rate of diet-associated diseases (Nestel, 1987). Moreover, some people eat 'rubbish' food despite nutritional education on what constitutes 'good' food. These people choose to eat food with negative moral and health-associated messages, suggesting that knowledge of cultural imperatives does not totally determine what we eat, and that we choose the food we eat for complex reasons other than simply nutritional value or cultural desirability.

Nutritional considerations, moreover, are part of a more general ideological framework in which diet is constructed. Commercial interests in the diet of consumers are often concealed in rhetoric about 'what is good for you'. For example, Wardle's (1977) study of the school milk scheme in the UK showed that milk was supplied to schools in an economic climate of falling milk prices due to a huge milk surplus. Medical research at the time confirmed that milk was valuable to children as a source of calcium and riboflavin. Despite this information, from 1971 the scheme was cut for purely economic reasons, not on the basis of nutritional knowledge or government policy based on health considerations. In Australia, the Whitlam Labor government terminated a similar scheme on the grounds that there was no evidence of general protein and calcium deficiency in children, claiming that children from poor homes drank more milk than their more affluent counterparts anyway. The Dairy Industry Marketing Authority established by the Wran Labor government in New South Wales some years later actively promoted the purchase of milk, targeting a teenage population with 'Moove milk', a flavoured milk advertised extensively on radio and television. Economic factors appear to have played a direct role in the contradictory history of the school-milk scheme. Government attitudes to children's milk consumption are determined by the economic interests of the capitalist economy in food production. Such economic interests mean that government and business use various ideologies at different times to support or rationalise changes in food supply. Medical research was used to justify arguments both for and against distributing free milk to children. The expert status of medical research was used to legitimise economic policy and influence consumption habits.

Variations in diet, however, are also a result of different local conditions of climate, soil, flora, fauna and the mode of production of food. National and multinational corporations have been motivated by profit to develop mass preferences for particular types of food, regardless of their nutritional value. Materialist–cultural explanations of food habits examine how the choice of food and the process of eating, as aspects of a social system, come to be regarded as an individual preference or even a problem (Harris, 1987). Societies are internally stratified in terms of rich/poor, sick/healthy, and different dietary habits within those groups indicate variations in status and power. Meat eating, for example, was associated in medieval Europe with the upper class, while the low-status members of that society subsisted primarily on legumes and flour (Goody, 1982).

Food and eating are often part of the way in which culture defines the status, power, duties and obligations of its members. In Stendhal's novel *Scarlet and Black*, published in 1830, Father Catenedes describes his rights at table in the rich parishes in the French mountain areas:

> There was much money, without counting the fat capons, the eggs, the fresh butter, and the innumerable other agreeable trimmings. And up there the curé [parish priest] is unquestionably the first man in the place—not a single good meal to which he isn't invited and where he is not lavishly entertained. (Stendhal, 1830:200)

The peasant in this account is obligated to feed the priest, despite possible food shortages: it is a matter of cultural duty.

In Australia before colonisation, Aboriginal hunter–gatherers had a diet which was rich in protein and included a variety of bush foods. L.R. Hiatt (1965) has argued that women were primarily the gatherers in Aboriginal society, and that men were important providers of food where gatherable foods were in short supply. This pattern was reversed where gatherable foods were plentiful; women then assumed importance as food providers. Food was distributed on the basis of relations of power, kinship and age.

The availability and development of technology is another influence on the quantity and types of food available to a society. Smoking meat and preserving food are types of household food technology that have now given way to the industrialised supply of food in supermarkets. Household-based ways of preserving food have diminished and consumers now live a long way from their food sources; we now depend on the food industry for supplies. People are less able to relate to the geographic areas from which their food comes and rely more on familiarity with the corporation that manufactures or sells it (e.g. McDonald's restaurants, Food Plus stores). National and multinational corporations now directly influence the quality and choice of food available in the highly urbanised West. The average supermarket offers the consumer about 6000 lines of stock compared to the corner shop's 600 lines. The apparent choice, quality and reliability of food-stuffs has increased, but the size of the market combined with rationalised production has reduced the number of brands of particular foods (Driver, 1983). By 1983 in Australia Permewan's Half Case and Franklins stores sold 45 per cent of all New South Wales groceries (Walker & Roberts, 1988). For the car-owning population, shopping now mostly consists of buying food at supermarket outlets. Food that is processed and packaged may contain potential health hazards from preservatives, chemical additives and toxins that develop as a result of the methods and duration of storage. The legally imposed standards of purity for food influence both what food is available for consumption and the economic aspects of production (Davis & George, 1988).

Food as language

The ways in which food is chosen, cooked and eaten are a function of implicit messages or food codes. A structuralist analysis of food assumes that food has ideological and symbolic functions. The association of these codes expresses a mythic logic in which cultural oppositions are described. Food preference and food habits are understandable in terms of food as a symbolic language, which unconsciously expresses fundamental cultural themes. Levi-Strauss (1965) developed a theory in which cuisine conveys messages through universal binary constructs: raw/rotten, cooked/rotten, raw/cooked, to form a 'culinary triangle'. He theorised that every culture's 'foodways' could be delineated within this structure. These binary oppositions, he claimed, construct myths which help individuals understand their place in their culture and in nature. According to Levi-Strauss, the way in which social events are organised around food and drink is part of an unconscious categorisation that belongs to all humans everywhere. Levi-Strauss's work has been criticised for its methodology (Harris, 1987), its generalisations (Lehrer, 1972) and the culinary triangle model itself (Goody, 1982). It has, however, had a significant influence on the study of linguistic categories and their relationship to food. Not only are food habits a reflection of qualities inherent in the food itself; food is also part of a system of 'signs' which expresses a language of symbolic meanings.

Eating particular types of food may be associated with notions of 'success' and 'failure'. The literature supports the assumption that advertising and the media influence people's attitudes to food and body shape (Chernin, 1986; Orbach, 1986). To be seen as successful in Western society, the individual not only has to have a particular body shape, but must also eat in a particular way. The successful woman is portrayed in the popular press as thin, fit and restrained in her eating habits. Advice columns in women's magazines tell women how to avoid 'pigging out' or eating in an unrestrained manner.

It is possible to use a semiological framework to describe food in a system of signification (Barthes, 1973). In his discussion of 'steak and chips', Barthes locates food in part of the binary opposites of nature and culture: 'Steak is a part of the same sanguine mythology as wine. It is the heart of the meal, it is meat in its pure state; and whoever partakes of it assimilates a bull-like strength' (Barthes, 1973:62). Eating meat is seen in Western society as part of a mythology of nature and culture whereby eating enables one to ingest animal-like attributes: by eating meat, males can become stronger. The meal can thus become a metaphor for an unconscious connection between food and beliefs about the world. In the early 1930s in New South Wales one such belief about meat eating was its association with producing superiority in the Anglo-Saxon race. Meat eating was believed to develop the supposed mental and physical superiority of white Australians over other races (Walker & Roberts, 1988).

Food taboos

Relevant to the construction of anorexia nervosa are theories of food taboos in the general population (as opposed to the population receiving treatment for eating problems). In Western culture, however, we may all be potential patients, subject as we are to complex and powerful food taboos.

Food can become taboo because of offensive smell, taste, appearance or some intrinsic quality or danger associated with its consumption. It can also become taboo as a result of learnt cultural attitudes. Disgust is often motivated by fears of incorporation of an offensive object, yet this disgust is learnt. Cultural beliefs about incorporation of food as a source of danger, or even the possibility that food can be changed in the stomach into something threatening, are found in some societies. Among the Cherokee people, for example, some believed that a witch had the ability to change food inside a person's stomach into an animal, or that ground snakes sprinkled onto food would lead to the growth of snakes in the victim's stomach (Hand & Stevenson, 1980). This cultural attitude to food taboos is similar to the situation of the happy toddler in Western society who will eat faeces but who learns disgust for this activity through the process of toilet training. Verbal and non-verbal messages from the parent communicate disgust to the child and the child thus learns what is socially acceptable to eat.

Fallon and Rozin's (1983) imaginative research into the ideational associations of a liked food with an item provoking disgust indicated that liked food would be rejected if associated with disgust items. Their American study found that individuals would not eat a soup they liked if it was stirred with a brand-new fly swatter. The subjects knew that the new fly swatter could not be contaminated; nevertheless they rejected the food they ordinarily liked. Rozin quotes a garage mechanic from Nebraska: 'A teaspoon of sewage would spoil a barrel of wine, but a teaspoon of wine would do nothing at all for a barrel of sewage' (Rozin, 1987:195). In comparison, Christopher Driver's observations suggest some British people make more tenuous ideational connections between what is consumed and its source. Commenting on the notoriously filthy conditions in some British cafes, Driver noted the 'British eating public's resolute refusal to make visual and imaginative connections between what is consumed and the source of it in field, slaughterhouse, pot and even plate' (Driver, 1983:103). Perhaps this is a healthy adaptation to local standards of food preparation, with the attitude of 'what the eye doesn't see, the heart doesn't grieve over'.

Many substances can make food disgusting, but if Rozin's (1987) observation is valid, no substance by its intrinsic nature has the capacity to make contaminated or disliked food likeable. Gaining or losing weight can give the body a socially approved appearance: the anorexic can change the body she believes to be disgusting into a so-called pure shape. Contaminated or disliked food, however, cannot be shaped into pure food by cultural processes.

Disgust and aversion can be associated in different cultures with social and religious attitudes unrelated to any physical risk in consuming the food. The hunter–gatherer diet of traditional Aboriginal people may include flying fox, goannas, lizards, bush rats and small reptiles, which set it apart from a diet acceptable to white Australians (Hiatt, 1965). The food taboos and preferences of white Australians have little in common with those of Aboriginal people before colonisation. One effect of colonisation has been an increase in poor nutrition and a progressive decline in Aboriginal health, which is demonstrably worse than the national average. The availability of a choice of Western foods has had little effect on improving the health of Aboriginal people.

Some sections of the Chinese, Melanesian, Hawaiian and African populations eat dogs. This is abhorrent in the West, where dogs are given names and protected by their owners. Similarly, breeding dogs such as the Chow for eating would seem disgusting to many Westerners. That reverence for the cow on the Indian subcontinent prohibits harm to an animal widely eaten in the West is ridiculed by some Western observers. Aversion to both the cow and the dog as food sources reflects individual food preferences influenced by religious and social attitudes. This is not to deny that in any culture some individuals go against religious or cultural mandates for various reasons and develop their own idiosyncratic food habits.

Fasting is another form of religious practice in which food may become taboo for specific periods. Jewish people, fasting on Yom Kippur is an affirmation of faith (Myerhoff, 1978). Similarly, specific foods are connected with various seasons of the Judaeo-Christian calendar such as Lent, when specific types of food are prohibited. Yet for many people, the avoidance of specific foods, such as meat, is not an expression of faith. Until the nineteenth century in Europe, few people ate meat. Access to such foods was difficult, even if it was desirable to consume them on 'holy' days. Fasting, in the Judaeo-Christian tradition, became a way of controlling desire and the temptations of the flesh. For Christians in Western countries, fasting is often part of a religious ideology, and is not classed as deviant or pathological.

Eating the superior food

Animal products have been perhaps the strongest site of taboos and cultural regulation. Eating meat is a way of ingesting the animal and can, on occasion, have gender-specific associations. The male may be described as 'red-blooded' and be fed red meat, while the female is served white meat (Twigg, 1984). In the UK some members of the working class consider 'good food' to be a cooked meal with meat. Meat is served to strengthen the male members of the family, and vegetarianism is often associated with 'women's food' (Twigg, 1984:27). In contrast, in Australia there has been a trend away from meat consumption. The decline is partly associated with the high prices of meat (Walker & Roberts, 1988). Illness food, or foods given to invalids, now have much in common with the diet culturally deemed appropriate for females—plain, bland food, and white meat (William, 1984). Poultry, once considered an expensive festive food, has, as a result of industrialised farming methods in the last 20 years, become a common, even a snack food. Chickens, on reduced feed, can now be slaughtered at seven weeks. (At one time, a growth period of 16 weeks was required.) Consumption of white meat by both men and women has increased as a result of changes in farming and marketing (Walker & Roberts, 1988).

Eating is part of the way in which people define themselves and are defined. Stricter control of food consumption, as a way of achieving health and vitality, has been advocated by numerous popular health-food advocates. Nathan Pritikin, Adele Davis and Dorothy Hall are among many proponents of an ontology of food and diet. Diet is said to contribute to physical and mental well-being. As Paul Atkinson (1984) has observed, the burgeoning health-food industry is one in which 'natural health foods' are opposed to 'unnatural, unhealthy foods', and people are encouraged by moral arguments to eat what is 'good for them'. The number of health-food shops in Britain grew from 800 nationwide in 1960 to 1200 in the 1980s, with a return of £80 million a year (Driver, 1983).

> The point about health foods as such, however, is that for the great majority of people these ideas do not actually lead towards a 'natural' or 'self-sufficient' way of life (whatever that might be in practice). They lead to minor adjustments in lifestyle. If anything, they substitute for action. In that sense the purchase and consumption of commercial health foods is a ritual, or magical act. Health foods can substitute for any major change in everyday life by allowing the consumer to ingest virtue in a concrete form. (Atkinson, 1984:15)

Mary Douglas believes, like Atkinson, that eating has intrinsic moral messages: 'good' people should consume certain types of foods. Her study of mealtimes was an attempt to demonstrate how meals express social values: social values tell us how to eat and what to eat (Douglas, 1984). Meals that 'good' people eat often express a moral message about the wholesomeness of the food or about the 'good' person's wholesomeness. Some see a vegetarian diet as morally superior to an omnivorous one.

The practice of vegetarianism, either by the woman diagnosed as anorexic or in the anorexic's family, has often been cited in the literature (Dwyer, 1982). Sheila Mac-Leod's account of her experience of anorexia includes references to her remote, authoritarian father, who was a 'health-food fanatic': 'All I can remember is that I didn't much like the food, but I ate obediently and probably out of fear of giving offence' (MacLeod, 1981:55).

Vegetarianism and health-food beliefs are often associated less with an avoidance of undesirable foods than with a positive intention to consume foods with superior qualities (Twigg, 1984). As Driver observes, vegetarianism is no longer 'the equivalent of wearing sackcloth and ashes' (Driver, 1983:106), but certain moral imperatives and codes continue to place the vegetarian diet both outside and superior to the more common omnivorous one. Dorothy Hall, in *The Natural Food Book* (1976), conveys this attitude nicely:

> If you happen to be the only person in the office eating raw carrots with a slice of home-baked bread for your lunch and drinking peppermint tea in mid afternoon, then you can regard yourself as the only sensible one present. (Hall, 1976:116)

The 'sensible' eater is set apart from the masses happily consuming their meat pies or Big Macs. Vegetarianism is at times advocated in emotive language: 'A butcher's shop is a commercialised mortuary . . . its violence is comparable to the violence of rape, murder and warfare' (*New Internationalist*, 1986:13).

To select a vegetarian diet associates food choice with moral stance. With increased use of supermarket shopping in Western countries and arguably more equal class access to different types of foodstuffs, people may express moral superiority to or difference from others through their ability to control their own diet and appetite. Practising restraint in the face of abundance or by adopting vegetarianism and other 'good' food habits are ways in which the individual might acquire certain moral attributes. Marion Woodman quotes 'Anne', a woman diagnosed as anorexic, saying:

> I preferred hardship games like war refugees or Anne Frank. On Sunday evenings I asked for cold beans out of a can. I always felt there was a conspiracy to keep my real identity from me . . . I was concerned to be good. (Woodman, 1980:76)

Some women may connect self-starving behaviour with a belief in the superiority of some foods and in restraint as a symbol of goodness. One vegetarian woman whom psychiatrists had diagnosed as anorexic told me, when she weighed around 32 kg: 'I can't eat any more. I am no good as a person if I don't keep reducing how much I eat.' Restraining appetite was for her the behaviour of a 'good' person. For some women, self-starvation can be an expression of moral strength and willpower.

Gender differences in diet

Women and children have unequal access to food in many cultures. The quantity and quality of food eaten by men and women reflects cultural values which give privilege to men. Studies of indigenous peoples in Malaysia and India by Bolton (1972) and Katona-Apte (1975), respectively, found that meat (protein) is restricted in servings for women and children. Meat is served first to males, who distribute it to other males, and then to women and children. The serving of meals can also indicate a gender-based division of labour—for example, in her role as caretaker and feeder of others the orthodox Jewish woman sees to males first, then women accompanied by males, and lastly single women. An orthodox woman may take food from another woman's plate to feed a man, but she will never do this to feed another woman (Myerhoff, 1978). As Catherine Berndt (1978) has argued in her Australian study, in some ways traditional Aboriginal women were in an enviable position, as their skills in food gathering made them independent from the menfolk when it came to the distribution of food. According to Berndt, the Aboriginal woman's digging stick was a symbol of her independence in food gathering.

Katona-Apte's (1975) Indian study, however, found that nourishing food is served first to males of superior status. Females in this population are often vegetarian, rationalising this food choice on religious grounds. Animal protein is the right of the highest-status member of the family—the male. With little meat available, the options for other family members become limited. This study also found a high infant mortality rate and cases of malnutrition among females. Injunctions to females to curb their appetite exist in some non-Western societies. In Bangladesh, pregnant women are able to indulge their appetites for sweets, sour fruits and various snacks. At other times, these women's low-status position would limit their opportunity to satisfy such appetites (Rizvi, 1986); if they did try to satisfy them they would be labelled 'greedy'.

The nineteenth-century illness category chlorosis (anaemia) was prevalent among some groups in the British female population. It was caused by insufficient protein and iron in diets that were considered acceptable for women at that time (Constantine, 1987:119). Bizarre forms of treatment were advocated for anaemia. In 1808 zomotherapy, the eating of raw meat, was recommended for the treatment of anaemic females (Muskett, 1908). In the more recent findings of the Australian Commission of Inquiry into Poverty (1976), a study of the diets of low-income families in Sydney revealed that iron was still the most common nutrient deficiency. Low-income families may suffer from iron-deficiency anaemia, which can be associated with reduced consumption of meat. If this is so, a significant proportion of women may be anaemic as a result of disturbing levels of poverty and protein-distribution patterns based on gender.

Diet and eating can be seen as a part of the self that people feel can be controlled by morals, healthy-diet information, cost, availability and medical mandates. Women in patriarchy are required to fill social roles that maintain their social inequality and their position as passive consumers, who buy and eat food in the correct, prescribed way. Part of their sense of self/identity may depend on their ability to demonstrate 'feminine' eating patterns.

Popular women's magazines may influence attitudes in the general public concerning body image, dieting and anorexia. In an article in *Cosmopolitan* (1988), a psychiatrist (a specialist in anorexia) was quoted as saying that men like plump women because they remind men of their mothers: 'They see a mother figure, both devouring and comforting. Most mothers are at the same time demanding and loving' (*Cosmopolitan*, 1988:120). In the dicta of dieticians, Health Department guidelines, health-food advocates and the medical profession, women are given specific messages about the meaning of their body weight. The implicit message from the psychiatrist quoted above would appear to be 'fat = mother', not the possibility that 'fat = sexy' or 'fat = lover'. The fat woman becomes the object of mother-love by the male; she is not seen as a seductress or virgin archetype in a patriarchal society.

Dieting has become an increasing obsession for many women. The biological urge to eat, together with an increasing availability of food, means that more people are required to exercise restraint in relation to food. As women fail in this, they try a variety of techniques for losing weight, including drugs, hypnosis, fasting, acupuncture, and the diets in fashion at the time. It is perhaps not surprising that anorexia nervosa is on the increase in Australia (Abraham et al., 1983).

A popular women's magazine asks readers: 'Is someone you know anorexic?' The list of warning signs given includes avoiding meals, losing weight, exercising daily, cooking for family but not eating herself. The reader is asked, 'Do you feel guilty if you eat a lot, or virtuous if you eat little?' (*Cleo*, 1987:97). A reader answering 'yes' to four questions may have an 'eating problem', says the magazine. The article is accompanied by a photograph of a white, middle-class girl aged between 14 and 16, looking bored as she gazes across a table of food. Individual habits and attitudes to eating become part of a biopolitical framework that includes a construct of symptoms. In this context, the well-dressed girl sitting at a table of food becomes an image of illness. Diet and eating can become a symptom (sign) that a suitably qualified medical practitioner can correctly interpret and label as a specific illness.

While self-starvation is certainly life-threatening, mortality statistics indicate that heart disease is the major cause of death in New South Wales. How is it that men with beer bellies, as they court death (according to the medical literature) by excessive drinking and eating, are not also generally referred to psychiatrists? The dominant discourses regarding the body position men and women in different places. Moreover, public messages about food appear to contain an essential contradiction. The consumer is encouraged to exercise strict control in the face of abundance and plenty: you can eat all you want, but you must also restrain yourself (i.e. not really eat all you want).

Anorexia has been called a 'fat phobia' (Crisp, 1974), whereby girls control their desire to overeat. As Garfinkel and Garner (1982) have observed, thinness in societies with an overabundance of food has come to be equated with the individual's ability to maintain self-control. Fatness in the Pukapukan society, on the other hand, is a mark of beauty and health in a society with few fat individuals (Hecht, 1985). In societies where food is less plentiful, fatness has been equated with high status. Restraint has much in common with the Greek concept of regimen. Philosophers such as Socrates exhorted their contemporaries not to give in to irrational pleasures of the body, but to practise moderation. Historically, common activities such as eating are interpreted as matters of health and ethics. The rational individual of today will therefore maintain self-control in the face of temptation, and show restraint in the face of abundance.

The prospect of pleasure, however, is promoted in the capitalist West to encourage consumption of goods and services. Excitement, fantasy and the symbolic power of consumption have cultural meanings associated with success and wealth (Davis & George, 1988). This indicates the complex and contradictory messages that the normal eater has to decipher. Women as shoppers make many consumption decisions for others and advertising is often directed specifically at them. Capitalism produces foods for profit rather than for their ability to improve health.

Economic interests promote the consumption of food of low nutritional value, if it is profitable. The foods the house-wife buys for the family, and the foods they consume, become part of a code of social meanings that is not inherent in the foods themselves. Buying and consuming are symbolic processes in which consumption becomes part of a person's self-image (Pringle, 1983).

Anorexia as a folk term

Individuals in any society can make sense of their eating habits by reference to the norms for diet and eating. These are given out to people through various discourses such as the discourse of aesthetics with its emphasis on culinary skill; the discourse of pleasure espoused by the gourmet; the discourse of ceremony with its emphasis on festivals and feasts, and the medical discourse. Individuals can then interpret their eating habits in terms of a biopolitics which is both pervasive and sophisticated. If, as Michel Foucault suggests, 'there is no power relation without the corre-lative constitution of a field of knowledge' then the field of nutritional knowledge forms part of a power dynamic, whereby people can be organised in relation to norms about diet, eating and weight (Foucault, 1977:27). Diet and eating, like sex, have an 'inexhaustible and polymorphous causal power', whereby irrational behaviour in diet can become part of a diffuse medical field of symptoms (Foucault, 1980:65). Individuals can then make sense of their and others' eating habits in terms of the 'truths' of this discursive knowledge.

When individuals move away from accepted social norms about quantity and types of food and when to eat, they may be labelled 'ill'. Clinical labels are ascribed by doctors. To make irrational consumption understandable, they posit it as a psychological disturbance that can be treated by psychiatrists (Davis & George, 1988). Individ-uals are able to select ideas about diet from the medical discourse and use them as a way of controlling their pleasures and those of others. Chips, tasty snacks to some, become 'things' and 'rubbish' and unacceptable to others. Attitudes towards food as temptation may originate in childhood, when liked foods are withheld by adults. This creates conflicting beliefs about, and attitudes to, food and diet in the normal population. Illicit and pleasurable consumption is opposed to obedient, boring, healthy consumption. Abraham and Llewellyn-Jones (1984) have reported that women receive messages that slim = successful and fat = failure. The young girl is expected to push aside the experience of eating as pleasurable and, above all, not get fat.

The anatomo-politics of the individual human body is linked to a biopolitics of the general population (Foucault, 1977). The supervision and regulation of levels of health, life expectancy and so on become the administrative concern of various disciplines, authorities and powers which aid the development of capitalism by adjusting populations to economic processes. The family doctor, for example, can become a source of medical knowledge and power who educates the family members in healthy lifestyle ideologies and dietary restraints. The privatised family in a capitalist economy is the ideal site for depoliticising interpretations of variations in food consumption. The development of a clinical and lay category 'anorexia nervosa' and its commonness as a folk term indicate that, in the private sphere of the family, various discourses inform the social consequences of private behaviour.

Different, new or adjacent categories for speaking about food are marginalised when statements about food are formed in a medical context. 'Anorexia nervosa' has become a complex combination of folk term and medical category. The term 'anorexia' is filtered to women through biopolitical channels, so it becomes a means of structuring and making sense of non-eating behaviour. People commonly overestimate their weight (Huenemann et al., 1966). During adolescence, concerns about fatness can be central to personality development. Dieting and weight reduction among the normal population is a result of conflict regarding gender roles, body image and values. This helps to explain how anorexia as an illness category has been popularised in the media.

Power and knowledge, as formulated in the dominant gender order, produce ways of speaking about dieting and femininity. Women diagnosed as anorexic accept anorexia as part of the objective truth of various discourses—including medicine—which position them within the male form of subjectivity. As Marilyn Lawrence has commented, hospital is, in effect, a place for the anorexic to learn new tricks. Television, film, newspaper and magazines similarly appear to be avenues for non-anorexics to learn about dieting, the symptoms of anorexia and how anorexics behave (Lawrence, 1984:82). Alternative ways of embodiment have been restricted or hidden by what is socially perceived as medical common sense. Perhaps the anorexic/self-starving woman selects the symptoms and behaviours which she presents to the doctor, who exchanges these for medical meanings about feminine embodiment.

Anorexia nervosa is now both a medical and a folk construct. The term has pervaded everyday speech and become part of a way of categorising self-starvation as an illness. Doctors become a central part of social process in which people make sense of diet, dieting and eating habits. The biopolitics is supposedly divorced from moral attitudes towards food, and is neutral, or scientifically legitimate.

The so-called anorexic is not simply a person with a problem about dieting and eating. She is part of a culture that, socially and symbolically, has made eating a problematic transformation of nature by culture. The creation of 'eating disorders' as an illness category, and the commercialisation of food consumption, place the eater, whether self-starving or 'normal', in a maze of food patterns, taboos and meanings. Anorexia nervosa and dieting are among the eating choices and patterns of food consumption in both patient and non-patient populations. The dieter is expressing cultural meanings and beliefs about food consumption and the biopolitics of food production in society.

2 Shaping conceptions of non-eating

The medical gaze and the construction of subjectivity

Having established the cultural context of anorexia nervosa, in this chapter I will trace the evolution of the 'illness' and the way in which it has been historically produced within medical discourse (which, as a discourse, has its own traceable evolution).

In examining the way in which Western medical discourse permeates everyday life and establishes norms for behaviour, including non-eating, the theories of the French philosopher Michel Foucault are helpful. Foucault shows how certain aspects of social behaviour, such as eating and non-eating, become transformed into areas of life subject to the authority of others. He describes this as a process of subjectification, where self-understandings of individuals are mediated by an external authority. In this process, medicine, for example, is a discourse creating its own objects of study (Foucault, 1971, 1973, 1978, 1979).

In *Birth of the Clinic*, Foucault examined the political, social and technical conditions which created a historical context for clinical observation (Foucault, 1973). By the eighteenth century, the mechanism of power in European society had changed from sovereignty, under which subjects were controlled by the visible power of torture, punishment by death and so on to a power of surveillance of the human body as the object of discipline. Medicine, by the eighteenth century, was the observation of disease in terms of symptoms and signs, and the classification of these symptoms. The symptom, which is the form in which the disease presents,

> is the first transcription of the inaccessible nature of the disease. Cough, fever . . . are not pleurisy itself—the disease is never exposed to the senses, but 'reveals itself only to reasoning'—but they form its 'essential symptom', since they make it possible to designate a pathological state (in contradiction to health), a morbid essence . . . and an immediate cause. (Foucault, 1973:90)

People are made objects of study of the discourse of medicine by various dividing practices and classifications of disease. 'Patients' are created by this discourse, which then analyses its own creations as objects of study. As this discipline developed, the 'patient' as a complete and single entity became less visible. By the eighteenth century, the opposition between mind and matter, subject and object, fact and value, was taken for granted as part of scientific medical discourse.

A political anatomy of the body is one in which the body becomes an object of power of various discourses, including medicine. The medicalisation of the body and health is produced in the following way:

> First certain behaviours or conditions are given a medical meaning—that is defined in terms of health and illness. Second, medical practice becomes a vehicle for eliminating or controlling problematic experiences that are defined as deviant (Riessman, 1983).

As doctors looked for signs and symptoms in their patients, the notion of norms of behaviour evolved. Abnormal behaviour, such as extreme dieting and non-eating, required its own forms of specialised, technical medical knowledge and treatments. This is part of the creation of a market in the community for medical expertise.

Foucault suggests that scientific disciplines such as medicine are also social practices. He provides a framework for understanding the process of subjectification whereby individuals understand themselves via the mediation of the external authority, in this case the doctor. In medical discourse, then, if the aetiology of anorexia could be discovered, it could be treated scientifically by the appropriate medical practitioner. The medical examination of the body is a means of objectifying the body, and a way of subjecting the body, and hence the patient, to medical surveillance and categorisation. The hospital was an ideal site for the medical gaze: here, the body was translated into a passive object of its own discourse.

Foucault's analysis offers a method of tracing how anorexia nervosa, as it is known today, was developed and shaped by medical knowledge and practices. Western medical discourse filters through our everyday life, and food, eating and dieting have become 'surfaces' on which emerge the so-called 'expert' fields of knowledge and power.

The development of medical discourse on anorexia nervosa

Medicine is more technical and specialised today than it has ever been. This specialisation makes it extremely difficult for the lay person to analyse it. In recent years there has been an increase in the study of medical knowledge and its relationship to the political and social environment (Freidson, 1975; Wright & Treacher, 1982). The process by which the human body has become an object of medical study and influence historically parallels a reduction in emphasis of the social and environmental contributing factors of disease. The dominant model of illness in Western society is one serving the needs of 'a consolidating class of professional physicians, marketing their "objective" clinical skills to a middle class clientele' (Comaroff, 1982).

Medicine in Western society, at least in this century, has traditionally portrayed itself as an objective, scientifically based discourse. This dominant paradigm places the focus on the mechanical aspects of disease, as opposed to patients' own understanding of their illness or disease. The scientific basis of medicine removes it from everyday ways of understanding disease and brings it into the domain of the 'experts', whose access to scientific knowledge and 'truth' overrides patients' own understanding of their body's functionings. The patient–doctor relationship is formed through an expert's understanding of the patient's experience of illness, via the disease model (Swartz, 1985). Diseases in Western society were considered to be biologically based entities, waiting to be properly analysed and identified by the medical profession.

Before the rise of the medical profession, fasting and food avoidance was at times regarded as a sign of miraculous powers or demonic possession. Bell's (1985) study of several hundred Italian female saints of the Catholic church suggests that fasting behaviour is as much related to social perceptions as to intra-psychic phenomena. Before the Reformation, fasting and food avoidance was regarded as the result of a saint's strong willpower and sense of sacrifice. Bell says:

> The mendicant emphasis on personal responsibility for salvation and its characteristic use of familial metaphor, as in the marriage to Lady Poverty, appealed to women in an especially direct way. It called upon them in the name of God and for their own salvation to take charge of themselves. Nearly half of the forty-two Italian women who lived and died in the thirteenth century and came to be recognised as saints exhibited an anorexic behaviour pattern. (Bell, 1985:149)

The fourteenth-century Saint Catherine of Sienna induced vomiting by pushing fennel stalks down her throat. Bell coined the term 'holy anorexia' to describe the medieval concern over whether this fasting behaviour was the work of God or the devil. The male-dominated hierarchy of the church determined whether the fasting nun was a heretic, a witch or a saint. After the Reformation, such fasting began to be regarded as insane or heretical behaviour. The concept of illness, rather than piety, became the explanation of women's ascetic practices.

In the traditional history of medical discourse, the progress and development of medicine was attributed to the genius and perseverance of the few great men who with their scientific knowledge were able to lead others out of ignorance and unhealthy practices. Social factors are diminished in this historical account, which privileged doctors with a special technical status and knowledge (Wright & Treacher, 1982).

Medical history, however, is not an inevitable progression toward the 'advanced' state of medical practice of today; it can also be seen as a history of discontinuity, whereby medicine became part of the ordering structures of the social body. It is in this context that we can map the 'discovery' of the condition anorexia nervosa, as noted in medical literature. It is usually attributed to Richard Morton who, in 1689, described two case histories in which a consumption, of mental origin, was characterised by loss of appetite, constipation, amenorrhea, overactivity and emaciation. This condition was not associated with fever or dyspnoea. Morton called it 'phthisis nervosa'. The disease entity had been 'found' and could now be codified and studied by the science of medicine.

The medical profession's interest in women's choice of non-eating developed further during the eighteenth century. Cases were reported in which anorexia nervosa was attributed to various disease factors, for example, a disturbance of gastric nerves (Naudeau, 1979). In 1868 William Gull published descriptions of anorexia nervosa in the *Lancet*. At first, Gull considered the condition one of 'apepsia hysteria', related to gastric nervous malfunction, but following the death of one of his female patients from starvation, Gull concluded that he was treating a psychological disorder influenced by neuropathological factors.

At the University of Paris, Ernest Lasegue described anorexia in his paper 'On hysterical anorexia' (1973), in which he indicated that the aetiology was hysterical in origin. ('Hysterical' women in another context were agitating for the unthinkable: votes for women. Some seven years before this, John Stuart Mill presented to the British Parliament a petition for women's suffrage with 1500 signatures.) The diagnosis of hysterical anorexia took place in a period when women were challenging their social role. Medical history is a history of symptoms which may be social in origin: hysteria in the nineteenth century; anorexia nervosa in contemporary medicine. Hysterical anorexia, Lasegue theorised, was related to gastrointestinal problems as well as being a form of mental illness. In the late nineteenth century in France, Charcot used hypnosis to demonstrate, according to scientific method, the psychological basis of hysteria, with anorexia as part of its symptomatology.

In Western society, the nineteenth century was characterised by an increase in the use of individual examination of patients, who could then be charged a fee for a scientific and moral explanation of their disease. The medical profession became more specialised, offering the public non-surgical methods of treatment as well as surgical procedures. As Gabbay (1982) has pointed out, concepts and categories within medicine and the sciences have changed over time. To the pre-Renaissance physician asthma, for example, was not a separate entity, but simply breathlessness. By the nineteenth century, authorities were describing the properties of 'pure' asthma:

> Turning then to detailed studies of individual concepts of asthma, we have seen how they might reveal even the most objective seeming clinical observations to be deeply rooted in, and formed from their author's general world-view, itself part and parcel of social, cultural and historical circumstances (Gabbay, 1982:42).

In the positivist approach to the history of medicine, solid facts are discovered and isolated from their social and political context (Figlio, 1977). Most medical history highlights the supposedly natural influence of the first observers of the so-called disease. The socioeconomic and political meanings of the disease, and the interests of the State in supporting or not supporting research and development of medical knowledge, are in the process obscured. Typhoid and cholera were among the epidemics which declined after the mid nineteenth century as a result more of improvements in social conditions, public health, hygienic practices and nutrition than of medical advances.

Physicians, however, are never a homogeneous group, and hold different opinions about the disease entities they treat.

Religio-medical alternatives to medical practice and its explorations continued into the eighteenth and nineteenth centuries in the forms of faith healing, mesmerism, homeopaths, hydropaths, and medical missionaries (Numbers & Schoepflin, 1984). Hydrotherapy, for example, was a form of treatment that, in the USA had by 1840 become a 'water cure craze', and a cure apart from the standard medical practices of the period. Its appeal was such that schools for hydropathic physicians were established, with graduates who claimed some technical advantage in the medical marketplace (Numbers & Schoepflin, 1984). The treatment was, however, dependent upon the administering hydropathic physician, and the initial, popular appeal of a cure without physicians was contained within a capitalist market via the so-called technical skill of the individual hydropaths. These healers, however, offered an alternative to the vigorous purges and bleedings of ordinary physicians and arguably provided a calmer, less aggressive form of healing, mostly without drugs. Some of the alternative healers sought to establish their legitimacy through the use of medical terminology and medical-sounding phrases such as 'homeopathic medicine', 'consultations', and 'herbal prescriptions'.

Studies of the medical perspectives on chlorotic (anaemic) girls in the late 1870s and in the early twentieth century illustrate how doctors used different theories to explain the 'green sickness'. Such work has drawn out the connections between class and the attributes of disease

(Figlio, 1978). In the nineteenth century, chlorosis was considered a form of anaemia specifically found among upper-class young women, although it was also evident among the working class. Explanations of its cause varied. Figlio argues that physicians' attribution of the disease to upper-class girls is an example of the way in which the middle class used concepts of disease to illustrate differences between the social classes (Figlio, 1978). The prevalence of chlorosis among middle- and upper-class girls was generally thought to be increasing. Its subsequent decline was attributed to various causes, including the reduction in blood-letting of expectant mothers and the association of chlorosis with iron deficiency. The development of the category 'anorexia nervosa' to describe self-starvation shows a similar pattern in its confusion of medical interpretations and its connection with adolescent girls in particular. These were young women financially dependent upon their families and with little power in society.

From body to mind: mental explanations of the cause of anorexia nervosa

By the early twentieth century, the medical classification of anorexia was still unclear. Karl Jaspers (1910) and Pierre Janet proposed that anorexia nervosa was a mental illness which could lead to schizophrenia or psychosis. Janet documented the case of 'Nadia', a young woman who would not adopt the traditional feminine role and was hyperactive and anorexic (Janet, 1907). Medical theories about the biological basis of this mental illness set the context for the search for the organic origins of non-eating. Morris Simmonds (1914) drew the debate over the classification of anorexia nervosa back into the realms of biology. He described the condition as panhypopituitarism—atrophy of the anterior lobe of the pituitary. This endocrinological origin was, he conceded, associated with psychological features, but the condition was not the result of mental illness. Named after him, 'Simmond's' disease was later treated with extracts from the pituitary gland injected into the non-eating patient.

The First World War brought the medical profession face to face with hysteria in male patients in the form of shell shock. Hysteria could therefore no longer be considered primarily a feminine disorder. Non-eating also became evident in males with shell shock, and no single organic explanation could be found for both the hysteria and the non-eating. By 1936, Ryle had further distinguished between Simmond's disease and anorexia nervosa by demonstrating the link between psychosexual trauma and amenorrhoea (Ryle, 1936). Sheehan (1939) also found that pituitary damage does not always lead to weight loss. The move away from endocrinological explanations for anorexia nervosa was paralleled by an increase in psychoanalytic interpretations of the condition.

In the prewar period the doctor–patient relationship was characterised by a view of the patient as the carrier of pathology—a docile body with a disease (Armstrong, 1982). In the inter-war years, the mental functioning of the patient came increasingly under the medical gaze. Patients' mental functioning was seen as relevant to their physical condition. The emergence of psychoanalysis in the 1930s, and notions of the role of the unconscious mind, led to the medical gaze being further extended to include aspects of the patient's personality.

Psychoanalytic explanations of self-starvation are part of a process of medical categorisation which removed the social factors of behaviour from the diagnosis and emphasised the intra-psychic origins of the illness. During the early twentieth century, psychiatry emerged from its institutional role as custodian of the insane. Before then, the asylum had been a place to contain the mentally ill and assist them by moral re-education. In the 1930s, in the area of psychiatry, ECT (electroconvulsive therapy) was developed and institutes for psychoanalysis established in Western countries. The development of a classification of diseases and mental illness, as well as theories such as Freud's, arose in a period of discoveries in pathology.

Success in isolating micro-organisms as causes of disease boosted lay confidence in the science of medicine and increased its social power and authority.

Psychiatry sought to establish its legitimacy in treatment by forming a close alliance with scientific biomedicine, specifically neurology. By 1934, the American Psychiatric Association had developed a joint board of psychiatry and neurology. The neurologist's task was to discover the organic basis of disease categories such as hysteria. Medicine as a discourse was attempting to isolate the factors specific to anorexia nervosa, both organic and psychological, so that it could determine the correct form of expert medical treatment for the non-eating symptoms of the often reluctant patient.

A common assumption in some psychiatric practice is that the social order in which it operates is free of contradictions (Ingleby, 1982). Powerful groups like the medical profession, however, have an interest in maintaining the status quo, in which normality is equated with sanity and correct diagnosis requires their specialist skills. The irrational, non-eating behaviour of the anorexic is made understandable by a psychiatric diagnosis which legitimises that profession's explanations and treatment. Yet, as Ingleby has argued, not all irrational behaviour is seen as mental illness in Western society. A fanatical devotion to one's country, for example, which can be just as life-threatening in wartime, is not seen as an illness. Psychiatry functions by 'adjusting the boundaries between sense and nonsense, but also by drawing the line between acceptable and unacceptable nonsense' (Ingleby, 1982:183).

It is interesting that 'Anna O', whose analysis by Breuer (1890) arguably formed the basis for the development of psychoanalytic method, was a so-called hysterical woman, a suffragette named Bertha Pappenheim. The patient, who was not eating, was diagnosed as having hostile feelings towards her mother rather than towards the representatives of the dominant gender order in society. In later life Bertha translated Mary Wollstonecraft's *Vindication of the Rights of Woman* and founded the German League of Jewish Women. Her symptoms before this public political life included anorexia and hysteria, and her treatment consisted of hypnosis and psychotherapy. Freud and Breuer had developed psychotherapy as a talking cure for hysteria which further individualised the melancholia of the illness. Social origins of the condition were obscured in a treatment which viewed hysteria as an individual problem.

The social order of the period was contradictory and full of tensions. In 1909 Miss Wallace Dunlop entered the British House of Commons and wrote on the wall a plea for women's suffrage. Sentenced to one month in prison, she initiated the first hunger strike as a means of gaining recognition as a political prisoner. She was released after several days. In subsequent years, the first wave of feminists increasingly used non-eating as a form of protest. The medical profession was unable to control this by force-feeding. Some medical practitioners no doubt justified their use of force-feeding by regarding the hunger strikers as hysterical, but the behaviour was not considered anorexic. The strategy of the hunger strike, which has been used by male and female prisoners in different cultures at different times, may have been particularly embarrassing to Western governments if the political prisoner was female and middle class—all the more so in a society like Edwardian England which believed in protecting frail, well-to-do women. No doubt working-class suffragettes were force-fed, but it was perhaps the image of the starving upper- and middle-class women that moved doctors to initiate force-feeding. It should be noted that, as Susan Bordo has pointed out, the anorexic's starving protest of today is *not* a conscious political act based on an understanding of the nature and source of her oppression, but rather a paradoxical and ambivalent attempt to obtain and conform to the socially constructed ideal body (Bordo, 1988).

The suffragette women of the early twentieth century were behaving in a manner that publicly challenged the dominant social structures. The militant public protests of the suffragettes in their struggle to win the vote, and the struggles of working-class women in the cotton trade unions in the United Kingdom as they organised factory gate meetings and enlisted union support for women's suffrage, were part of the social and political context in which the medical category of anorexia nervosa was being developed (Liddington & Norris, 1978). Medicine in the private sphere could control self-starvation in women; in the public arena, the social body was less able to be contained and controlled.

The most commonly accepted psychoanalytic interpretations of anorexia nervosa developed after the 1930s were based on the following general premises: Eating disorders represent an oral disturbance formed in the patient during her first year of life. In this period, the mother–child relationship is of primary importance to the child's development. The infant may develop unconscious feelings of resentment at not receiving sufficient nurturing from the mother. The psychoanalytic theorists argue that the infant defends against her oral ambivalence at not having her needs met with feelings of anxiety and guilt. Hunger, in analytic theory, is the infant's experience of need for care by the mother, or the ego's experience of dependence upon nature for survival. If the mother does not satisfy the hungry ego-needs of the neonate, then according to this theory the basis of anorexia nervosa, as latent pathology, is established.

Anorexia nervosa was further developed as a disease entity by theorists such as Anna Freud (1958), Thoma (1967), and Waller, Kaufman & Deutsch (1940), who proposed psychoanalytic theories of non-eating, in which the patient defends against oral receptive wishes by starvation. According to these theorists the anorexic starves herself as a way of suppressing her 'real' hunger, which was not satisfied by her mother when the anorexic was a child. She feels unconscious resentment towards her mother and displaces it onto an alternative object, food. The anorexic is demonstrating that she does not depend on others and is self-sustaining.

Phenomenological theorists of anorexia nervosa such as Binswaanger (1944) and Kuhn (1953) interpreted the condition in terms of the way the anorexic patient experiences her bodily needs. Roland Kuhn suggested that the anorexic patient's primary relationship with her parents forms the way in which she learns to process and understand the body's physiological need for food and her experience of hunger and appetite. He postulated that 'spatio-temporal protophenomena' are perceived differently by anorexic patients than by the normal population. His treatment involved a reorientation of the patient to 'normal' concepts of space and time. I do not propose to discuss the relative merits of these theories in detail, but rather to use them to illustrate the wide spectrum of medical interpretations of anorexia nervosa.

In the psychodynamic school, M.S. Palazzoli (1965), one of the most influential theorists, believes the origin of anorexia lies in an over-protective mother, who rewards the anorexic's compliance. The patient's body, in psycho-dynamic terms, becomes associated with her mother, and her own ego functioning is depressed. Inability to recognise the needs of her own body, and its association with a threatening object i.e. the mother, results in an ego threat to the patient. At puberty, the patient re-experiences earlier ego-repressed material. Theorists can, however, change their viewpoints. From 1974, Palazzoli adopted a 'family-systems' approach to anorexia nervosa. She now emphasises the interactions and communication difficulties within the anorexic patient's family instead of individual treatment. Like Salvador Minuchin et al. (1978), she practises an approach in which the anorexic girl is theorised as having strong feelings of loyalty and as functioning in a covertly enmeshed family which is unable to manage conflict. Anorexia is a way of dealing with the conflict the anorexic girl feels about achieving her autonomy. Palazzoli has characterised the anorexic patient as 'mentally alert, energetic and receptive, except in the terminal phase. Anorexia nervosa invariably involves an active and deep wish to lose weight and reluctance to seek help' (Palazzoli, 1974:31). The theoretical system may be different, yet the patient is still reluctant to submit to the medical gaze. As Palazzoli herself observes, the patient is usually a minor whose treatment is paid for by her parents, and the patient submits to treatment in order to avoid the threat of hospitalisation, not through free choice (Palazzoli, 1974).

Anorexia is most frequently reported among adolescent girls, who, because of their economic dependence on their parents, are brought in for diagnosis and treatment. Anorexia among older women who are independent may escape the psychiatric system, as such women may choose to refuse or avoid treatment.

Hilde Bruch (1976), whose writings have also had great influence, sees anorexia nervosa as caused by the patient's failure to perceive her internal cues of hunger, as a result of her greater need to comply with the needs of her mother. In this theory, perception of appetite and hunger are regarded as learned behaviours. The anorexic patient has learnt to be more responsive to others' perceptions about her needs than to her own perceptions. Anorexia nervosa is therefore regarded as a communicative disorder.

The psychoanalytic approach is currently used to treat so-called borderline anorexics, or anorexics in recovery, often in conjunction with medical treatments to ensure the patient achieves a minimum weight level and maintains that weight. The intra-psychic emphasis of psychoanalytic theory individualises the self-starver in her struggle with non-eating. Whether the 'disease' is attributed to orality, unresolved Oedipal issues or the expression of a borderline personality disorder is disputed in the analytic community. Nevertheless, the techniques of psychoanalysis, such as the analysis of transference, and interpretation of the individual's resistance in therapy, are seen as a relevant part of psychoanalytic medicine which can be used to treat the self-starving woman.

Current medical definitions of anorexia nervosa

The medical literature on anorexia nervosa generally agrees on the physical aspects of the disease. Bliss and Branch studied 300 cases at random from the literature and found the following indicators of anorexia nervosa:

a   The average woman classified as anorexic weighed 112 lbs prior to malnutrition. Twenty-one per cent of all patients had a final body weight of 60–70 lbs.
b   Body fat was less than 20% of total body weight.
c   Age of onset; late teens to early twenties. (Bliss & Branch, 1960:46)

Poor nutrition is also associated with the symptoms of hypothermia, hypotension, toxic encephalopathy and abnormal biochemistries including low serum potassium levels. When the body is starving it adopts a conservation state in which the pulse falls and body temperature and blood pressure drop. Schwartz and Thompson's (1981) longitudinal study found that 6 per cent of patients with anorexia nervosa die. Baker and Lyen (1982) estimate the death rate at between 0 and 19 per cent J.P. Feigher et al. (1972) have developed the most widely accepted set of criteria for a diagnosis of anorexia nervosa:

A   Age of onset: prior to 25.
B   Anorexia with accompanying weight loss of at least 25 per cent of original body weight.
C   A distorted, implacable attitude towards eating, food, or weight that overrides admonitions, reassurances and threats.
D   No known medical illness that could account for the anorexia and weight loss.
E   No other known psychiatric disorder.
F   At least two of the following manifestations.
(1) amenorrhoea (2) lanugo (3) brachycardia (4) periods of overactivity (5) episodes of bulimia (6) vomiting (may be self-induced).

In Vandereycken and Meerman's (1984) recent clinician's guide to anorexia nervosa, patients are seen as having both biological and psychological problems. Anorexia nervosa is described as a depressive illness characterised by biomedical abnormalities and positive results on dexamethasone suppression tests; this is used to indicate and support the theory of the organic basis of the disease. Families with an anorexic member are reported as having a high rate of affective disorders, and antidepressants are recommended for the treatment of the anorexic patient. Despite agreeing on the common signs and symptoms, the medical profession interprets the meaning of non-eating in a variety of ways:

> Typically the adolescent anorexic will worry about obesity and diet excessively to escape the ridicule of family and friends. The hysteric will develop somatic disturbances which interfere with the ingestion of food. The phobic will fear obesity and refuse to eat. The obsessional will ruminate about food and obesity, pursue a diet ritualistically and may indecisively fluctuate between bulimia and abstinence. The depressed patient will lose his appetite and develop a disinterest in food, whereas the schizophrenic will develop delusions about food and most typically decide it is contaminated or poisoned. (Bliss and Branch, 1960:46)

The medicalisation of non-eating enables some doctors to slot their patients into diverse categories, from 'hysteric' to 'schizophrenic'. Research into the prevalence of anorexia nervosa has been extensive in the last two decades. Nylander, in Scandinavia (1971), for example, found that one in 150 adolescent girls studied was anorexic, and 80 per cent of women in the general population had dieted by the age of 18. In Australia, women have a greater tendency to diet than men. In a recent South Australian survey, 43 per cent of women were found to diet, although 34 per cent of the dieting women were not overweight by Australian standards (Crawford & Worsley, 1988). Russell (1970) and Crisp (1974) describe anorexia as a 'fat fear', with a diagnosis in terms of psychological features only. In the United Kingdom, one in every 200 girls under the age of 16 studied by Crisp, Palmer and Kalucy (1976) was anorexic. Friesh (1977) attempted to link menstrual abnormalities with anorexia nervosa. He found that menstruation ceased when the proportion of body fat fell below a certain necessary level in anorexic girls. Ganner and Garfinkel (1978) studied non-eating in ballet dancers and models, and found that anorexia can be a result of social and vocational pressures.

Many researchers suggest that the prevalence of anorexia nervosa is increasing (Garfinkel & Garner, 1982; Palmer, 1980; Bemis, 1978). This may also reflect an increase in the number of anorexics seeking medical help, or an increase in the frequency with which psychiatrists diagnose the condition. Schwartz, Thompson and Johnson (1982) stress the sociocultural factors that contribute to the development of anorexia nervosa. The majority of anorexic patients, they found, are young women who are white, middle-class, and high achievers. These studies indicate the current diversity of medical opinion on the self-starving woman and the extent of medical interest in her behaviour.

These diverse studies are part of a context in which non-eating becomes merely a symptom of an illness, which can then be used to explain behaviours in the patient. The woman who starves herself may be choosing to abstain from food for many varied reasons which are not included in the current definition of the illness category anorexia nervosa. As Georges Mounin (1985) has suggested, medicine as a field of knowledge is in general agreement in measuring observable facts, but the aetiology, nosology and psychopathology deduced from these symptoms may change in medical discourse over time. The biomedical aspects of anorexia have been extensively documented but the theories drawn from these 'facts' are both extensive and contradictory.

Medicine has a closed view of women's bodies and minds: it sees women as passive patients who consume medical services in disproportionate numbers (Gove and Tudor, 1972). Women are more frequently diagnosed as having mental disorders than men are (Busfield, 1983). The dominant gender order in Western society creates the possibilities out of which women find explanations and meanings about embodiment.

In summary, then, medicine now regards anorexia nervosa as a psychologically based disease with specific physical symptoms (Feigher, 1972). Treatments for anorexia are diverse. There are both short- and long-term treatments within all the major theoretical schools of psychiatry, psychotherapy and medicine. Non-eating has become a form of 'illness behaviour', which places it within the domain of the medical profession. This abundance of theoretical approaches, however, has been unable to improve the prognosis for women diagnosed as anorexic.

Medical discourse on anorexia nervosa is mostly blind to the political and economic factors influencing women. The disease model of psychiatry ties self-starvation to an illness model in which reluctant patients will continue to find themselves in costly treatment, often at their parents' behest and against their will. It is against 'reason' in Western society to starve oneself, and the self-starver finds herself rendered 'reasonable' in society as 'the anorexic patient'. The anorexic in this discourse is someone who needs to see a psychiatrist and may be hospitalised.

Some women do starve themselves to death. In the face of this tragedy, their families and medical professionals are at a loss to say how these women at the extreme end of non-eating behaviour could have been helped. Psychiatry shapes our understanding of self-starvation, despite its lack of a unified theory of treatment or of proven success in the cure of anorexic behaviour. Those diagnosed as anorexic are managed by psychiatry, but not always cured. Self-starvation by women can be placed in the context of the social and cultural meanings that non-eating has for women, and of the position of women in the dominant gender order. Such a political anatomy reveals the ways in which women's bodies have become the object of medical power and knowledge.

3 Feminist interpretations of anorexia nervosa

The medicalisation of women's bodies

Anorexia nervosa is part of a process of medicalisation of women's bodies that has gradually assumed authority over how women are embodied and hence how they embody themselves. In this process, the social aspects of illness are obscured, and disease becomes something over which medical science can assume authority. Certainly both men and women's bodies have been the subject of medical treatment, but in studying anorexia, my interest is how medicine constructs women's bodies. In the process of medicalisation, the female body becomes the object of a medical gaze and discourse which reconstitute it as a body subject to normative medical criteria according to universalising medical principles. The view of the body thus becomes a restricted, closed medical view.

In Australia in the late nineteenth century, married women had an average of seven children. High infant mortality and miscarriage rates meant that women were pregnant more often than this figure suggests (Mathews, 1984). Until recently, the hazards of childbirth and gynaecological complications meant a decreased life expectancy for women and high infant mortality rates. In some parts of Europe, professional guilds of midwives trained apprentices and maintained high standards of care for pregnant women, while others practised outside these guilds with dubious effects. By the eighteenth century, the emerging medical profession had gradually taken over the role of the midwife and local healers, treating not only upper-class women but poorer women as well. It was in the interest of the new medical professionals to reduce the influence of midwives and local healers and consolidate their own power and field of knowledge. Male midwives and surgeons assisted at births in upper- and middle-class families, and there was some competition over fees for service (Donnison, 1977). These male practitioners, because of their knowledge of the use of surgical instruments, could assist in difficult births, and many developed expertise in this area. In the domain of childbirth, female practitioners such as midwives, who worked unregulated by medical concerns, were supplanted by mostly male medical experts. The church in Western society had fashioned many of the sexist notions of the female body and reinforced male dominance over it. By the nineteenth century the medical profession had become part of this process and of its attempts to control female reproduction and regulate sexuality.

Leavitt (1984) quotes an American physician in 1870 as saying: '. . . the Almighty, in creating the female sex, had taken the uterus and built a woman around it.' It is debatable whether this attitude was widespread, but it is an example of a medical attitude which defines women's primary function as reproductive—woman by nature is her uterus. Her social role is thus a direct result of her ability to reproduce.

During the eighteenth century, anatomical models were used for teaching purposes in some French medical schools. As Jordanova has observed, the female models were displayed lying down in a passive sexual pose, while the male models were standing, often in positions suggesting activity and movement (Jordanova, 1980:54). Medical schools thus treated the physiological aspects of the female body in a sexualised manner. This sexualised attitude became part of a medical discourse which incorporates sexist and moral attitudes in the supposedly neutral study of anatomy.

Ehrenreich and English have argued that women in the eighteenth and nineteenth centuries were regarded as frail creatures, whose behaviour and activities were curtailed by medical mandates presented to them as benevolent concerns for their well-being. The apparently frail female could not be a healer or rival practitioner to the male, but was suitably qualified to become the patient and thus the consumer of the male's services (Ehrenreich & English, 1973). This analysis has been criticised as tending towards biologism and depicting women as a homogeneous group of passive victims of stereotypical expert male doctors (Jordanova, 1980). At times women are victims of the medical experts, but generalisations such as Ehrenreich and English's do obscure the fact that women can to some extent choose both doctor and treatment.

During the twentieth century, the closed, medical view of female sexuality underlies some biomedical research into the physiological basis of sexual activity. In the search for a 'real' objective biology of sex, hormones, neurological centres in the brain, orgasmic contractions and so on have been studied in an attempt to codify male and female sexuality according to medical science. Following from this, the American Psychiatric Association in 1980 listed female 'anorgasmia' as a form of psychiatric disorder. A woman's ability to have orgasm was therefore assumed to be within the medical domain and thus susceptible to treatment by the psychiatric profession, rather than an unregulated, non-medical matter and the concern (or not) of the woman herself.

In the medical literature, women's minds have been closely linked with their reproductive organs; it has been assumed that femininity and maternal personality traits could be managed by the correct medical treatment of those organs. To the Victorian medical practitioner, a woman's reproductive organs were the most important parts of her body, and functioned effectively only when their limited energy was not dissipated in other activities, such as work and study. Medicine in the eighteenth and nineteenth centuries was a science of 'hydraulic mathematics' (Turner, 1985:219), in which the body's inputs and outputs could be regulated by moral discipline to achieve a socially desirable equilibrium. Scientifically based medical discourse reinforced social structures and their oppression of women. Some nineteenth-century middle-class women were advised not to pursue higher education on the grounds that it would injure their health. Standard nineteenth-century medical texts described menstruation, pregnancy and the various normal stages of female development as 'critical periods', during which women were vulnerable to serious permanent damage and therefore in need of medical supervision (Morantz & Zschoche, 1984). According to the medical model of this period and its system of dynamic equilibrium, the doctor restored the female body to a state of balance. Views of the female body in which such functions as sexuality and reproduction were unregulated and not in need of medical intervention were displaced by the closed, medical model of the body.

The Victorian physician was in a position to decide whether a woman suffered from a genuine medical problem which could be treated or whether she was a malingerer attempting to avoid her duties and established roles. The defective uterus could be treated by the surgeon, while the defective mind, influenced by the female anatomy, could be treated by the psychiatrist. Medicalisation renders the 'sick' dependent; doctors mediate 'sick' people's exemptions from normal duties as well as expectations of their behaviour (Riessman, 1983). To some extent this mediating role lingers in some medical practice today.

Importantly, a shift in medical discourse from a moral to a disease base may mean that a patient diagnosed as having anorexia nervosa, for example, is regarded as suffering from a 'disease', and not from some inherent weakness of character. While some psychiatrists may practise in a moralistic manner, the disease model has recontextualised explanations of the causes of madness from the moral to the scientific. This has mixed benefits for the consumers of health care, men or women. Once a medical view of the body has been established, so-called deviant behaviour can be constructed as a symptom of an illness, which can then be diagnosed and treated by doctors (Mathews, 1984:20). Individuals are thus not held responsible for their behaviour.

The mental condition perhaps most frequently attributed to middle-class women in the Victorian period was hysteria, a condition so nebulous as to subsume such divergent symptoms as neurasthenia, hypochondriasis, depression, schizophrenia, violent seizures and apathy. To the nineteenth-century physician, the hysterical middle-class woman was the embodiment of femininity. Smith-Rosenberg's (1972) study of American women of this period outlines the inconsistencies between ideals of female social behaviour and the real world in which American women lived. The ideal woman was dependent and gentle, a follower. The ideal mother was expected to be self-reliant and a caretaker of the family. It was a contradiction within which many women struggled to find a sense of identity.

Hysteria was often 'found' in women overwhelmed by pregnancies, children and household management. In the early part of the nineteenth century, the hysteric had to have a hysterical fit to be diagnosed, but by mid century the fit was no longer considered essential pathology. The medicalisation of women's bodies and minds did not require violent overt symptoms such as fitting, but could presume expertise over more subtle forms of behaviour and label them, too, as symptoms. As Smith-Rosenberg observes of this period:

> The medical profession's response to the hysterical woman was at best ambivalent. Many doctors—and indeed a significant proportion of society at large—tended to be caustic, if not punitive towards the hysterical woman . . . These patients did not function as women were expected to function . . . (Smith-Rosenberg, 1972:663)

In common with self-starving women today, the hysteric woman could have a vague mixture of symptoms and was treated by a diversity of medical treatments, according to the differing theories about the causes of hysteria.

Feminist theory and anorexia nervosa

Feminism has challenged the medical profession for its lack of understanding of the gender issues in anorexia nervosa and has attempted to set up an alternative explanation of the condition. Feminist criticism assumes that no account or theory is neutral, and that the political implications of theory and methodology must be studied. This challenges male-dominated discourses which are presented as neutral on gender issues. Feminist theorists argue that a diagnosis of 'anorexia nervosa' is not an apolitical judgment but one which indicates the tensions inherent in the dominant gender order.

The principal feminist theories about anorexia have been developed by feminists working as therapists—Kim Chernin (1986), Susie Orbach (1985), Marlene Boskind-White (1979)—and influenced by feminist philosophers and theorists, for example Simone de Beauvoir (1949) and Juliet Mitchell (1974). These writers need to be considered in the context of feminist theory on subjectivity—specifically French feminist theory—which addresses the non-biologically based aspects of gender. Simone de Beauvoir was influential in developing a feminist discourse of the female body and the oppression of women. She pointed out the dialectic in culture and the individual whereby the male is regarded as the norm, the positive subject, and the female is set up as the inessential object, defined in relation to the male. Consciousness for de Beauvoir is the site for the opposition between the male subject and the female object. The male is defined independently of the female. Woman's identity in culture, however, is found in her status as other. De Beauvoir sees woman's body as a social construction, the 'inessential other; an object incapable of acting as the meaning-giving subject' (de Beauvoir, 1949: 29). For her, the meaning of the female body in society is determined by its reproductive capacity: 'Woman, like man, is her body; but her body is something other than herself' (de Beauvoir, 1949:60–61). De Beauvoir drew attention to the nature of the oppression of women, which is in part a result of the way in which women's bodies are constructed by culture. In patriarchal culture, woman is alienated from her body, as the female body is not the subject which gives meaning but rather the object of a cultural view which is masculine. A woman's body thus becomes something apart from herself.

In her analysis of the role of the unconscious, Juliet Mitchell (1974) described the means by which women internalise their oppression. Although critical of elements of Freud's theory (for example penis envy, rather than envy of the privilege of male status) (Mitchell, 1974:179), Mitchell uses Freud's concept of the unconscious to explain the mechanism whereby the dominant ideology about women and their status is reproduced. She regards the unconscious as the site where women come to terms with their status as the 'inessential other'. This internalisation of oppression in women's unconscious influences their conscious perceptions of the possibilities and opportunities available to them in life and of their ability to act in the world.

Nancy Chodorow's *Reproduction of Mothering* (1978) was the precursor to Orbach's and Chernin's studies of anorexia from a feminist perspective, and drew upon the work of Balint, Winnicott and Freud to focus upon individuation as the core of gender identity. In psychoanalytic theory, separation or individuation is the process whereby infants gradually develop a sense of their existence as separate from their mother. Chodorow placed girls' attempts at individuation in the context of the social aspects of family life within a patriarchy. She used Freud's concept of the pre-Oedipal period to explain the more fluid ego boundary between the daughter and her mother in early childhood, and the daughter's consequently weaker gender identity. (In contrast, the son more readily separates from the mother and develops a sense of his gender as different from the mother's.) Chodorow regards a girl's femininity as a function of her attachment to the mother: the girl's sense of identity is based on how others perceive her rather than on an inner sense of difference from the mother. In adulthood, then, a man's self-definition is based on his experience of being separate, not intimate, and different from the mother. A woman's ability to achieve this inherently male sense of self is limited and, Chodorow might argue, creates the basis for such problems as anorexia. As Sheila MacLeod observed about her own experience of self-starvation: 'It seemed obvious to me at the time that to be a child was safer and easier than to be an adult and that, specifically, to be a girl was safer than to be woman' (MacLeod, 1981:78).

Feminist theorists drawing upon 'object relations theory' could point to the gender-formation period of the pre-Oedipal stage as one during which the girl's sense of identity is founded on her attachment to her mother. This attachment creates difficulties for the young woman in her search for individuation; the anorexic girl has not been able to break this infantile primary bond. She experiences an extreme version of feminine identity formation in which either her normal, relational ego is exaggerated and she defines herself as that which she has lost, or her sense of self is incomplete.

Kim Chernin (1986) argues that the origins of anorexia lie in the young woman's potential capacity to develop past her mother in the world. The daughter develops guilt about her mother's condition—'a mother whose life has not been fulfilled and a daughter now presented with the opportunity for fulfillment' (Chernin, 1986:43). Chernin presents the mother–daughter bond, cemented via food during infancy, as the storehouse of intense infantile fantasies. She goes so far as to attribute the eating disorder to a 'Kleinian memory' of wishing to bite and tear at the mother: '. . . I wish to suggest that we have not known exactly how to account for the extremity of these feelings because we have neglected the Kleinian fantasy life of the pre-oedipal period' (Chernin, 1986:120). According to Chernin, the anorexic woman's guilt and anxiety can be understood only in terms of her desire to inflict, and her sense that she has succeeded in inflicting, oral attacks on her mother.

Why, then, are there so few male anorexics waiting to bite the nipple that fed them? Drawing again upon Klein, Chernin argues that the male is able to fantasise attacks upon the female body (not himself) and is therefore not as vulnerable to self-destructive rage as the adolescent girl. The girl's fear of appetite is linked to her fear of anger and of expressing anger. The primal association between mother and food makes the girl's struggle to separate from her mother a struggle with guilt over her own growth at the expense and to the diminution of the mother.

> For the male, ability to discharge primal rage at the mother through aggressive fantasies of attack upon the female body, without at the same time incurring the danger of attacking the self, clearly gives men a powerful advantage in managing rage. And it frees them from the self-destructive behaviour that arises so conspicuously at the turning point of a woman's life. (Chernin, 1986:129)

Chernin argues that the anorexic woman, unable to control or express her primal rage towards her mother, directs her anger inwards to harm herself. That is, her fear of anger towards her mother is displaced onto food and eating.

As Swartz (1987) has commented, Chernin's interpretation to some extent portrays the woman with an eating disorder as a martyr to social injustice: '. . . through observing and sympathizing with her struggle the reader will be demystified about society as a whole' (Swartz, 1987: 616). In *The Hungry Self*, Chernin suggests that communication about identity does function through food, but she emphasises the mother–daughter relationship and food:

'They [anorexics] tend to explain their mother's life as if they themselves, from earliest infancy, drained and depleted the mother with the intensity of their needs' (Chernin, 1986:64). She argues that the mother–daughter bond and struggle create a predisposition in females to anorexia nervosa. The eating problem is an opportunity for the mother to feed the daughter; for the mother and daughter to relive symbolically and unconsciously the weaning period, when the infant believed that breast-milk ceased because of her own oral aggression or aggressive fantasies and that breast feeding drained vitality from the mother. Chernin does not address the question of anorexia nervosa in women who were bottle-fed as babies, nor how the prognosis for anorexic women and girls might be improved by this emphasis on the mother–daughter bond.

The mother–daughter dynamic is also a theme in Susie Orbach's work. She argues that women's insecurity about their bodies is culturally induced. Orbach's anorexic is a heroic figure: 'Like a hunger striker, she is in protest against her conditions. Like the hunger striker she has taken as her weapon a refusal to eat. Not eating is her survival tool' (Orbach, 1985:131).

The young woman is seen as symbolically linked to her emotional needs and her inability to have these needs met. Anorexia, according to this view,

> is an attempt to be adequate, good enough, pure enough, saintly enough, sufficiently unsullied to be included and not rejected. It is an attempt to represent and exemplify the values of that world and through such conformism find acceptance and safety. (Orbach, 1986: 103)

Like Chernin, Orbach regards anorexia as a defence against dependency needs. The anorexic learns from her mother that she will not be able to get her emotional needs met nor be active in the world; she must serve the needs of others. Orbach says the anorexic's mother is also under pressure to have a slim body, and keeps a watchful eye on her daughter's appetite. The daughter learns at an early age (six months to three years) that her dependency needs will not be met, and finds separation from the mother difficult; her separation/individuation process is therefore scarred.

Orbach sees eating as a 'combat zone' where the object of desire (food) is associated with fear and with concepts of good and bad. In *Hunger Strike*, published after her popular *Fat is a Feminist Issue*, she attempts to assist professionals in 'clinical interventions' (Orbach's words) and anorexics themselves in self-help. I agree with Orbach that the starting point for feminists is the oppression of women, that feminist psychology reflects a 'preparation for this [oppression] and a rebellion against it', and that each individual woman's psyche embodies patriarchal social relations. It is important, however, that feminists exercise caution in their use of descriptive medical categories such as 'anorexic women' or 'the anorexic' (Orbach, 1986:130).

The 'I' of Orbach's text is the sympathetic, enlightened clinician (Orbach, 1985:127). Orbach's main theoretical influence is psychoanalysis, particularly the British school of object relations. She extends Winnicott's concept of a 'false self' to that of a 'false body', in which the child, lacking the chance to experience a body whose physicality is good, develops a false body as a defence against the non-accepted real body. Changing the shape of the 'false body' is a way for the self-starver to reshape her prime social asset as a woman—her body. That she reshapes it in a parody of the feminine ideal suggests that the control of her needs and appetite is a major source of her sense of identity. Orbach argues that the anorexic is a strongly conforming girl who has taken society's injunctions about the embodiment of femininity to their extreme.

The process whereby the 'anorexic' is created and its selective aetiology, are not clear from Orbach's analysis. Not all conforming girls are anorexic. Why is this so? The mother–daughter relationship is problematic for many women and it would be of interest to survey the so-called normal population to see how adequately they believe their dependency needs were met. Parenthood, moreover, is often a haphazard career—meeting a child's needs can be affected or interrupted by economic exigencies, as well as psychological predispositions. It is difficult to regard the mother–daughter relationship in isolation from the broader social forces that also shape the family.

Marlene Boskind-White's (1979) feminist theory of anorexia differs from other feminist interpretations. She postulates that sexual fears, which predispose women to anorexia, result from an inordinate fear of rejection by potential male partners and the fear of being unable to meet men's needs. She argues that women are socialised to dependency and are often unable to establish a sense of self. Bulimarexics, a category Boskind-White coined, exhibit a combination of anorexia and bulimia rather than belonging to two distinct illness categories. Bulimarexics have a 'disproportionate concern with pleasing others, particularly men, a reliance on others to validate their sense of worth. They have devoted their lives to fulfilling the feminine role rather than the individual person' (Boskind-White, 1979:438).

Feminist theories such as Boskind-White's appear to offer a sophisticated reinforcement of the medical view. They assume that there are women with specific disease entities or illnesses which can be relabelled along feminist lines to render existing knowledge more meaningful. This attitude is evident in Orbach's account of her therapy of 'Audrey', aged 26, whom she saw for two years. Orbach describes how Audrey gave up her anorexic behaviour when she understood it was a much-needed defence against exposure of her original, negative object relations. Many feminist therapists are speaking *for* the self-starving woman, albeit in an attempt to set up an alternative discourse. It is rare in any analysis of anorexia nervosa to hear the voice of the woman who is being treated for anorexia.

In 'What is an Author?', Foucault argues that the truth of a discourse lies in the strategies which it brings into play, not simply in what it says (Foucault, 1979). It is not enough, he argues, to measure the value of a discourse in terms of what it explicitly states as truths. A discourse should also be evaluated in terms of the possibilities it creates for particular types of thought or action. Foucault considers Marx and Freud to be founders of discursivity in that their writings are never declared to be false, nor their theories invalid. Writers within a discourse establish their own theoretical validity in relation to the work of the discourse's founders. In this way the subject of the discourse does not become its originator but is analysed as a variable in the discourse. Foucault's question in relation to a discourse, is 'What difference does it make who is speaking?' (Foucault, 1979:160). The voice of the woman who starves herself is rarely heard in the literature on anorexia nervosa. Instead others speak about her and for her.

One of the major problems for feminist theorists is that we describe the oppression of women and the limits of medical discourse and then proceed to discuss the woman and her symptoms within parameters drawn from that discourse. Feminist clinical practice must address the political and epistemological implications of these theoretical notions. Boskind-White, for example, obtained many of her subjects by placing an advertisement in a university newspaper. It described the symptoms of anorexia and offered a feminist support group to respondents—who presumably selected themselves as fitting into this illness category. Subjects were given questionnaires on bingeing and fasting behaviour, early childhood training, and so on. Boskind-White reported that the feminist support group was a success, but not how this success was measured.

Feminist theoretical approaches to anorexia nervosa generally agree that the dominant patriarchal gender order creates an enormous chasm between women's experience of self and the cultural and social mandates about what they can and should experience. Anorexia nervosa is theorised as a symptom that symbolises the oppression of women generally.

Critiques of this feminist analysis and its use of psychoanalytic theory have come from Marxists such as

Elizabeth Wilson (1987). Wilson is critical of feminist psychoanalytic theorists such as Mitchell for remaining silent on the question of what political action women should take against their oppression. Moreover, she says, the treatment of lesbians and homosexuals in psychoanalysis should be, and is not, challenged. Lacanian feminists fail to contest the traditional conformist role of therapy with its emphasis on adjustment to the dominant gender order. Some feminist therapy is criticised for placing emphasis on the individual woman instead of encouraging changes in society through political action.

There are indeed major divisions within psychoanalytic theory and debates within analytic circles as to the meaning of femininity (Rose, 1987). Similarly, feminist therapists are not a homogeneous group, and feminist theorists and therapists differ in theoretical views and therapeutic style. Their single point of commonality may be in their attempt to show how women in the West have been excluded from male knowledge and their positing, in turn, of women's place in that knowledge.

Feminist critical scholarship on anorexia nervosa, I believe, needs to be considered in terms of the questions raised by Foucault's work. How can feminists challenge the power structures of male-stream knowledge without at the same time becoming entangled in reductionist concepts of the object, i.e. the anorexic? Orbach, Chernin and others have attempted to increase the knowledge about anorexic women in the face of male knowledge that has mostly omitted considerations of gender and power. While this may challenge the discourse within psychiatry, psychology and sociology, it does not challenge the fundamental assumptions about the form and function of these discourses themselves.

Foucault has described the manner in which power and knowledge operate in a mutual relationship to define reality. Knowledge about subjects and objects in culture is a function of a totalising process which accumulates information on particular groups in society e.g. the anorexic, and then defines reality for that group (Foucault, 1982:

213). How is it that there is a single, unitary group of women with ascribed symptoms who are called 'anorexics' and analysed by feminists? The totalised object, 'the anorexic', becomes netted down by some feminist theorists and therapists. Feminists establish their credibility to speak about 'anorexics' through their work as psychotherapists or counsellors of these women. It could be argued that this is a different manner of challenging the hegemony of male knowledge, yet it employs means similar to those of the dominant male theorists. Feminist theory, that is, assumes that 'anorexia' exists as a discrete entity, and that it can be re-codified from a feminist perspective—thus giving feminists the right to blow the whistle on the treatment of 'anorexics' and offer an alternative treatment for the totalised 'anorexic' object.

Authorship, according to Foucault, gives the writer certain rights and privileges. The authority even of a critical knowledge exerts power over the object of that knowledge. Certainly therapists approaching anorexia nervosa from a feminist point of view hope to help the self-starving woman understand that her individual problem is part of the oppression of women generally and a function of power imbalances between the genders in society. Yet feminist theorists and therapists could benefit from a strategic use of the Foucauldian understanding of the process of totalising an object—in this instance, 'the anorexic'. We must be careful not to get caught in the juggernaut of speaking *for* the woman being treated for anorexia, who is seldom the originator of the discourse, but is instead its silent object.

4 Theorising subjectivity

Language as a means of conceptualising the self

Feminist theorists' analysis of women's role and position in society has been influenced in recent years by the theories of, among others, Freud, Jacques Lacan and Michel Foucault. Feminists have challenged Western philosophical assumptions about what constitutes truth, knowledge, power, mind and body, and the politics of desire. Theories on subjectivity can be useful in evaluating patriarchal discourse as it constructs femininity and women's embodiment. The term 'subjectivity' refers to the individual's development of a sense of self. Discourses produce conditions from which our subjectivity is positioned. A woman with anorexia, for example, is not only that. She may also be a sister, daughter, unemployed woman, student, wife, suicidal girl or patient. Each role has associated with it different meanings, positions and ways in which the individual woman makes sense of her self in her subjectivity.

Language is relevant to a discussion of subjectivity and the construction of the self: it is a way of constituting and ordering meaning for individuals in society. The experience of 'the self' for women in Western society is contradictory, since the female body is represented in a way that maintains the sociopolitical status quo. Language, full of socially engendered images of women's bodies, creates the possibilities from which women think and speak about their embodiment as women. The woman diagnosed as anorexic is caught up in a chain of signification. It is in the process of the lay and medical diagnosis of anorexia that she is given ways of thinking about what is happening to her. Women make sense of the weight loss by means of a diagnosis or way of thinking. This diagnosis is expressed in a language which has a limited range for the feelings, thoughts and intuitions that might be outside the diagnosis. Anne, a 22-year-old woman treated for anorexia nervosa, describes her experience of silence in the discourse: 'I think I cannot go on. The tide comes in. There's no meaning . . . there's no meaning . . . there's no meaning. The third time it goes right over me. I can't find my relationship to God and all the world recedes. All meaning suddenly drains out of life' (Woodman, 1980:78). How is the woman being treated for anorexia to find meaning outside of the lay and medical discourse that defined her? Without an analysis of the way language constitutes meaning in society, a discussion of self-starvation in women does not acknowledge the functions of, and conflicts inherent in, women's embodiment in a patriarchy.

Theoretical developments in anthropology, philosophy, language and writing, such as the work of Ferdinand de Saussure, challenge the traditional notion of language as a neutral vehicle for thought. Saussure argued that words function as signs which produce sound and concepts. In our culture it is conventional to refer to women who self-starve as 'anorexics'; it is possible, however, to refer to them with other terms, such as 'fasting women' or 'self-starvers'.

To rename women referred to as anorexic would not challenge the conceptualisation of the problem as one specific to a particular, homogeneous group. Yet the label 'anorexic' is not neutral. It carries with it implications for the way in which people so defined understand themselves and their behaviour. The language we speak creates the possibilities from which we can conceptualise ourselves. The study of semiotics, or signs and their relationships, can give insights into how individuals learning speech and language are also learning a structure by means of which they will develop their sense of identity. The sign is both a linguistic and a philosophical problem.

Structuralists have posited that meaning is produced through binary oppositions such as nature/culture, masculine/feminine through structural relationships rather than logocentric meaning. Logocentric philosophy, the dominant Western philosophy from Plato onward, maintains that knowledge is neutral. Reason proceeds in an apparently ineluctable logical progression to the so-called facts. In contradiction to this, Levi-Strauss, de Saussure, Benveniste and Jacques Derrida have indicated that a study of signifying systems can help to uncover the relations of myths, words and concepts which, when put together, produce meaning. Meaning is conveyed not simply by the definitions of the spoken word, but also by the words which are not used. The process of locating contradictions within a text, for example, makes it more than just a literary work to be passively read—it may also reveal signifying practices of hierarchical phallocentric thought implicit in that text. Phallocentric thought assumes that meaning is found only in relation to the bearer of the symbolic phallus. Sense of the world is made from the position of the man who speaks for both man and woman, and from a hierarchical perspective which places men at the top of the symbolic order. Hierarchical phallocentric thought is possible because of the absence of an alternative. The subject becomes embedded in or eaten up by the discourse. The world is no longer chaotic but controlled, measured and weighed. This discourse excludes the understandings and voices of women.

Structuralists and post-structuralists have elaborated theories about the rules which govern the production of meaning. They ask how meaning is possible for individuals and under what circumstances individuals can articulate their own meanings, relevant to the construction of self (Derrida, 1967; Barthes, 1971; Benveniste, 1971). Individual consciousness is made possible by notions of difference. The speaker becomes the subject, or 'I', of the language in order to formulate meaning. Consciousness of self, according to Benveniste, relies on language to establish differences between 'I' and 'you'. The sense of individual self thus depends on the formulation of the 'non I'. Language operates within a metaphysics of meaning (Benveniste, 1971).

It is in the exposure of the essentialising fetishes 'truth, femininity, the essentiality of women or feminine sexuality' (Derrida, 1982:70) that Derrida and the post-structuralists have most to offer an analysis of the ways people create meaning from signs of illness:

> ... what if we were to reach, what if we were to approach here (for one does not arrive at this as one would at a determined location) the area of a relationship to the other where the code of sexual marks would no longer be discriminating? The relationship would not be a-sexual, far from it, but would be sexual otherwise. (Derrida, 1982:76)

Women who self-starve have been subject, as are all women, to contradictory messages about their position within society and culture. In the dominant gender discourse, a woman becomes irrational or mad if she is unable to reconcile the contradictions in her identity formation. As Sheila MacLeod found in what she describes as the depressed period of her anorexia:

> I 'chose' anorexia rather than mental illness as a defence against confusion. But towards the end of my anorexic period I think I was verging upon mental illness ... I had become out of touch with reality as perceived by others and unable to cope with demands of everyday life. I had begun to feel that there was some sort of glass partition between me and the rest of the world. (MacLeod, 1981:106)

All women are bound up by the code of sexual marks which are discriminating and contradictory. MacLeod distinguishes between mental illness and her anorexia. In her formulation of meaning in relation to non-eating, the 'I' is anorexic and the 'non I' is mentally ill.

Lacan and subjectivity

Lacan's theories about the connection between the unconscious and ideology can be applied to an analysis of self-starvation in women and of women's embodiment. Lacan points out that in psychoanalytic theory, women are regarded as symbolically lacking. Feminists have also been influenced by his re-reading of Freud's Oedipus complex and his theory of the way in which sexuality is engendered (Mitchell, 1974, 1982); (Lemaire, 1977). In Lacan's psychoanalytic theory, it is with the acquisition of language that we enter the symbolic order: the organisation of culture and society which creates within it the position of the subject. For Lacan, sexual identity is perceived by the split subject in relation to a world that conceals the unconscious. Lacan's theory conflicts with those of ego psychology and object-relations psychoanalysis. Object-relations theorists suggest that gender identity is biologically based and is developed through the individual's interaction with external objects. Lacan refutes this.

Lacan's re-reading of Freud also extends understanding of the way in which language keeps the father (male) dominant in culture. Referring to the symbolic father—The Name of the Father—Lacan elaborates how the mother indicates her positive regard for father over baby. In his analysis this is not the actual father, but a paternal metaphor. Through the medium of language, the individual enters the symbolic order, in which men are dominant, as is the male view of the female body.

Developing Freud's concept, Lacan sees the unconscious as being 'structured like a language' (Lacan, 1972: 139). He theorises that the unconscious contains pre-linguistic signifiers. In the early months of life, when the child cannot speak, it has no sense of separation from the 'other': the boundary between self and 'other' is vague. The mouth, voice and so on orientate the newborn to the world in a sensual manner. For Lacan, the 'imaginary' is the register of images conscious or unconscious, perceived or unperceived. The imaginary is analogous to Freud's concept of the pre-Oedipal period. In the move to the imaginary order, the child starts to experience itself as having a unified body, instead of being a collection of separate objects. The individual is not some innate entity, some discrete self that will ultimately be a solidified whole. According to Lacan, then, individuals are initially fused with other outside objects including the mother—the object of desire. Identification with the object (mother) creates the sense of self. The inner sense of part-objects is counterbalanced by the introjection of the mother.

According to Lacan's theory of the mirror stage, the child experiences a split between the self and the object of desire, the mother. It acquires a sense of unity and identity only through a relationship with a discrete outside entity— the mother (Lacan, 1977:1; Lemaire, 1977:79). The individual is then able to differentiate between self and other in the symbolic order. The mirror is Lacan's metaphor for this stage of psychic development. For Lacan, identity is not achieved through the development of the ego, but through a developing sense and awareness of the 'other'.

Recognition of difference—in the Oedipal phase, absence of the penis—is a precondition for the girl child to enter the symbolic order. As language requires a perception of gender, individuals must acquire a gender identity in order to resolve the Oedipus complex and speak. Gender acquisition becomes the desire to achieve a relationship with the lost object (mother) in the form of another person.

Lacan argued that the issue of the Oedipal period is not castration *per se*, but castration of the symbolic phallus (signifier of desire). The father perpetuates the symbolic order by depriving the mother and child of the ability to satisfy their desire. As Irigaray has commented on Lacan's interpretation, the symbolic phallus becomes a signifier of lack:

> The ceaselessly recurring hiatus between demand and
> the satisfaction of desire maintains the function of the
> phallus as the signifier of a lack which assures and
> regulates the economy of libidinal exchanges in their

double dimension of quest of love and specifically sexual satisfaction. (Irigaray, 1985:61)

That is, woman asks to be desired—for that which she is not. The signifier of desire is located in the body of another. To resolve the Oedipus complex the child must repress the experience of wholeness with the mother.

According to Lacan, then, to become female necessitates acceptance of a definition of femininity as the absence of masculinity. The girl in the imaginary and symbolic processes becomes a deficiency that can be filled by the desire to have a baby. Her body is phallicised and she becomes the pleasurer of the man–father. It is difficult in Lacan's account to see the feminine as anything but mediated by the male. The symbolic phallus becomes the means for structuring human subjectivity for both men and women. Lacan's construction of subjectivity is similar to Freud's: 'Consider in this regard, that anorexia is so specifically a female symptom that it can be correlated with the girl's inability to accept her sexual "destiny" and can be seen as a sort of desperate rejection of the sexual blossoming to which she is fated' (Freud, 1953:250).

Personal identity for Lacan, then, is only acquired through the acquisition of language which in turn relies upon the acquisition of gender. The sense of self is developed according to a patriarchal symbolic and social order. Important to my analysis of self-starvation in women and of their embodiment is the notion that with the acquisition of speech, the child enters society and formulates its sense of self in terms of that society. The implications for women with anorexia are seen, for example, in the sex-role ideology of the social order, which places women under pressure to conform to a particular weight and body style. The acquisition of gender and language requires acceptance of definitions of gender and sex roles that may be inherently restrictive. Gender acquisition may involve a desire to fit the female body into the socially acceptable mandates for weight, without any acknowledgment of difference in embodiment or social roles.

Lacan's theory implies that the unconscious has a strong influence on our sense of self and on how we think about our en-gendered bodies. How individuals think and speak about their bodies is part of a symbolic order in which women are defined not for themselves, but in terms of their position in relation to men.

French feminists and Lacan

Some feminist theorists have investigated psychoanalysis partly in the hope that it could provide some explanation of the psychological resistances to personal change shown by people in oppressed groups in society, including women. French feminists created the theme of woman-as-other—'difference'. Their theory emerged from a critique of Freud and Lacan, and an analysis of subjectivity and the psychological mechanisms whereby gender inequalities are reproduced (Marks & Courtivron, 1981; Moi, 1985). The work of Luce Irigaray and Hélène Cixous illustrates concepts valuable to any discussion of subjectivity and language.

Irigaray extends the concept of difference to develop a positive image of femininity. Using psychoanalysis in a strategic way, she shows how gender identity is socially constructed through language. Her *Speculum of the Other Woman* (1974) is an extraordinary and controversial exposition of women's oppression via language and representations of the female body. In it she describes the phallocentric bias of Freud and Western philosophy, with their emphasis on sameness. Psychoanalysis, she says, defines both men and women in reference to the male, and thereby reproduces the structures of gender power.

Irigaray's description of the way in which the male becomes the 'subject' and the female becomes the 'other' is relevant to my discussion of the construction of women's embodiment. Irigaray points out how men speak universally for men and women. It is language that directs individuals in their orientation to the world. Subjectivity and meaning expressed in language mirror patriarchal power relations. A patriarchal symbolic order inscribes women's bodies with limited possibilities and restricted access to the dominant gender hierarchy.

Irigaray suggests that Freud and Lacan emphasise vision and male ways of perceiving the world. For example, the little girl sees she is castrated. Patriarchy defines the female as not having a phallus, as in Freud, or as non-masculine, as in Lacan. Woman's identity, then, is predicated upon a perceived lack of a phallus rather than a possession of her own sex. Yet according to Irigaray, the female body could also be conceptualised in other ways, for example, via touch instead of vision (then the lips of the female genitalia touch each other while the penis is dependent upon contact with another). The male needs an instrument to know himself, and sublimates this in language (Irigaray, 1974). Irigaray points to a different construction of femininity whereby the pre-Oedipal unity with the female is not repressed but continues into the next stage, so that the possibility of a new language and logic emerges. A woman's femininity would then be constituted by her relationship to her own body and to her mother's body, instead of to the masculine. Irigaray seeks to subvert the dominant ways in which women are presented to themselves in society.

Women's silence in history is a silence of her double lips, born of the need to silence both her speech and her sexuality. The double lips are a textual metaphor to suggest a different entrance to the symbolic. Irigaray develops the concept of 'jouissance', or female playful pleasure, which, unlike male pleasure, is the gateway through which women speak in their own voice, with their own lips. 'I see the lips as the entrance to female sexuality . . . All holy texts mention a threshold, to me the lips of a woman are that threshold. The entrance to the house. The entrance to intimacy' (Irigaray, 1985:195). Irigaray is not suggesting some sort of anatomical positivism, but a challenge to the dominance of phallocentric symbolic.

The rejection, the exclusion of a female imaginary
certainly puts woman in the position of experiencing
herself only fragmentarily, in the little structured
margins of a dominant ideology, as waste, or excess,
what is left of a mirror invested by the (masculine)
'subject' to reflect himself, to copy himself. (Irigaray,
1977:30)

Attention to the silences in patriarchal discourse may
create, I suggest, the space from which women can develop expressions of femininity and glimpse strategic interventions hidden in those silences and margins. These may
conflict with the dominant social processes of subjectivity
and its construction. The silence is 'that-which-was-passed-
over-in-the-silence' (Derrida, 1982:67), or the aspects of the
situation that were observed and were not spoken or could
not be verbalised. The body that a woman may choose not
to feed is not only a physical body with the attributes of
abnormal blood chemistry, anaemia, lanugo and so on, but
also a symbolic and cultural product of an ideology.

In her novel *Cardboard* (1989), about her experience of
anorexia and her treatment in Australia, Fiona Place
describes the connection between anorexia, speech and
language:

[The doctors'] desire to influence, I would suggest,
extends far . . . to cover their desire they use a language
which denies subtexts.
refuses to flirt,
to admit
to the hidden
And it would seem to me that any language that denies
subtexts must be diminished in its capacity to effectively
treat illness. Especially anorexia nervosa which I believe
is first and foremost a language problem . . . why
couldn't I be real. Why couldn't I use the words I heard
other people use, and think the way real people thought.
(Place, 1989:97)

Place illustrates the implications for women of the
exclusion of a female imaginary. Unable to find words,

the writer experiences herself as un-real; not a real person. The woman in the patriarchal symbolic is defined only in relation to the male (the subject), who is the real person. It is hardly surprising that women feel un-real and silenced in their struggle to come to terms with unconscious drives and social mandates concerning acceptable behaviour. Irigaray presents women with the possibility of a multiplicity of concepts: woman who is not man and not subjected (Berg, 1982). But this remains problematic until the female ceases to be the male's symbolic mirror image. 'I, too [a woman] am captive when a man holds me in his gaze; I, too, am abducted from myself. Immobilized in the reflection he expects of me. Reduced to the face he fashions for me in which to look at myself' (Irigaray, 1981:66).

In Irigaray's reading, Freud and Lacan define 'feminine' in terms of deficiency; a negation of the male. When the little girl accepts that she does not have a penis, she rejects her mother (all women) and seeks the father in order to attain the symbollic phallus, the powers of the male sex (Irigaray, 1974). Irigaray explores the ways in which the feminine is defined as a lack, a negative image of the subject in Western culture, a silent subject. Women, she says, have been 'misinterpreted, forgotten, variously frozen in show cases, rolled up in metaphors, buried beneath carefully stylized figures, raised up by different idealities . . .' (Irigaray, 1985:144).

This observation of patriarchal ideology is also made by Hélène Cixous. Writing in a strongly metaphorical way, in *The Laugh of the Medusa* (1976), and *Castration or Decapitation* (1981) she pushes the binary oppositions of masculine and feminine. Drawing on her experience of women who are at the edge of culture, the madwomen, Cixous suggests that with their bodies women support the realm of the proper (heterosocial society, patriarchy). To challenge the 'proper' is regarded as madness within a patriarchy:

. . . without the hysteric, there's no father . . . without the hysteric, no master, no analyst, no analysis! She's the unorganizable feminine construct, whose power of producing the other is a power that never returns to her . . . She is given images that don't belong to her, and she forces herself, as we've all done, to resemble them. (Cixous, 1976:47)

Woman's body and sexuality have been repressed and shamed into love of another's body, not her own female body. Cixous urges women not to remain within psycho-analytic closure and advocates a return to woman of the body that has become for her an 'uncanny stranger on display' (Cixous, 1976:250). Language is the mechanism by which women's bodies become a reflection of woman as 'other'. Woman's body is made a stranger to her by the language that perpetuates the dominant position in society of men and male views.

. . . isn't this fear convenient for them? . . . isn't the worst, in truth, that women aren't castrated, that they have only to stop listening to the Sirens (for the Sirens were men) for history to change its meaning? You have only to look at the Medusa straight on to see her. And she's not deadly. She's beautiful and she's laughing. (Cixous, 1976:255)

These French feminists offer alternative ways of understanding femininity. They provide strategies for the emergence of differences in women's embodiment, and for a change in language. In a feminine imaginary, women could explore their potency, strength and power. This imaginary could be based in the pre-Oedipal feminine, but it need not be. A fluid femininity in which the expression of sexuality and eroticism is possible may be part of a way to deconstruct the feminine body. A feminine imaginary may offer women unconscious images which could, in culture, create for them different ways of embodiment.

However, the importance Irigaray and Cixous place on the connection between the feminine and the pre-Oedipal period does have at times elements of an essentialism of the female body. Not all women experience 'jouissance' in the same way. Women experience their femininity in varied ways, depending on their position in the hierarchical society and their race and class. The daughter of middle-class parents who is diagnosed as anorexic and treated as an in-patient for two years in a private psychiatric hospital is presented with a different model of female normality from that of her working-class colleague. The middle-class girl is presented with a passive model of femininity in which she must place herself in the hands of the experts until she is cured. She is not enjoined to an active model of femininity. The working-class girl diagnosed as anorexic is often prescribed psychotropic medication, and returns to work as part of her rehabilitation. She has only periodic stays in hospital. Without private health insurance, the working-class 'feminine' that she is constrained to adopt cannot afford to be developed by costly long-term psychiatric treatment. Hers is an active model of femininity: she must rejoin the workforce and benefit from short-term therapy.

The implication of an exploration of language as the means of conceptualising the self is that the woman who is labelled anorexic is expressing herself in a language which is not neutral. The meaning she finds for her weight loss is part of a lay and medical discourse dominated by male meanings. Psychoanalytic theory such as Lacan's gives an explanation of how ideology in the unconscious affects how we think and speak about ourselves. Language and the entry into the symbolic are based, for women, upon the adoption of a male view of the female body. Irigaray and Cixous challenge patriarchal ideology by proposing a feminine imaginary and a plurality of femininity. A deconstruction of femininity helps in understanding 'anorexia nervosa' as part of the code of meanings in Western society. This code links the feminine body—and its representation in culture—to a construction of knowledge which places women in a subordinate position in society and, at the same time, depoliticises gender and embodiment.

5 Thinking about femininity

Self-starvation and meaning

Language and cognition indicate a different epistemology for women and men as they are presently en-gendered by society. Language and communication have a relationship to conceptions about the world that is not simply representative but involves complex ideological and philosophical issues. Women are unconsciously taught in culture a text that can be read as 'anorexic'. They interpret that text in society as a sign of an illness—an illness which places them within the domain of a medical and lay discourse about anorexia.

In an examination of anorexia it is necessary to draw out the connections between individuation, the unconscious, and the way in which knowledge is constructed whereby one gender and its body shape are given preference over the other gender and body shape. Gender, size and mass are commonly assumed to be discrete entities that can be studied as part of a discourse in male-stream thought. Femininity, however, is not simply determined in a moment on the basis of genitalia, but develops over time in the process of gender acquisition and attribution in society.

One woman, diagnosed by a physician as having anorexia nervosa told me, 'If I didn't have anorexia, I'd have something else. I've always been unhappy with myself, with my body.' Here anorexia is a lay term which expresses a continuum of positions—from the deeply distressed woman who is hospitalised to the woman who, in response to stress, finds herself adopting and presenting the set of psychosocial problems that is currently deemed culturally appropriate and promulgated in the popular media. The woman quoted indicates that there was a certain degree of choice in her adoption of anorexia. If anorexia is a desire for the so-called ideal body, how do women think, speak and find meaning in relation to their body as it is inscribed by culture?

If the majority of illnesses of women are indeed illnesses about gender dependency, then a greater prevalence among women of anorexia nervosa, depression and agoraphobia is consistent with oppressive patterns of subjectivity (Turner, 1985). Diagnostic procedures and treatment may present the self-starving woman with a conversion to male meanings. These meanings remove her from any sense of her self that differs from the meanings enshrined in male ideology.

Psychiatrists traditionally arrange data in terms of deviation from the norm, i.e. in terms of pathology. Diagnosis involves matching symptoms and signs with knowledge about established disease entities. A diagnosis of 'normal' occurs in the absence of pathology, rather than in the presence of some indicators of health. A well-known study by I.K. Broverman et al. (1970) claimed that mental health clinicians associated 'normal' adult healthy behaviour with stereotypical male traits. If women are to be seen as healthy adults they have to assume the stereotypical attributes of the mentally healthy man. Differences in communication frames between female patients and male doctors generate an inevitable tendency for doctors to find pathology. The woman diagnosed as anorexic is then described in a language (the clinician's) which equates 'healthy adult' with 'healthy man'. The possibility of a woman's experiencing anorexia nervosa is as much a result of her place within language and patriarchy as it is an indication of her 'pathology'. Differences and inequalities in power, knowledge and gender in society position the individual as subject and create tensions in the subject's experience of self.

Given that the woman who self-starves has, on some level, a choice—eat or starve—her ambivalence about her choices as woman-in-the-world suggests a sense of self that changes, a matrix of unconscious desires, and dominant gender discourses that give power to one type of body over another. Moreover, her context is generally complex —food consumption is problematic for many in Western society. The woman who self-starves attempts to find meaning and understand her behaviour as it is reflected back to her—from a masculine mirror of meaning. For the self-starver to see herself in a mirror which is not fashioned by male subjectivity, to speak in a language which codes female ways of knowing, would require a fundamental challenge to the dominant gender order, which privileges one type and shape of body over another.

The medical profession has thoroughly documented the physical aspects of 'anorexia'. Yet despite its considerable efforts to cure anorexic women and girls, it cannot predict a cure with any certainty. Neither does the medical literature offer clear indications or agreement about the most valuable forms of treatment. Medicine relieves some of the suffering of women with eating problems while at the same time obscuring the social and political aspects of their diagnosis and treatment. It views the individual woman as an isolated 'case'. It is not helpful for women to consume services that promote a universalised world view in which they are disempowered and in which one method of therapy assumes authority over others. Moreover, evaluations of treatment for anorexia such as Agras and Kraemer's (1984) find that no one treatment consistently produces an improved outcome, nor has treatment outcome improved over the past 50 years. This being the case, it would seem unwise to promote any one form of treatment as the answer for anorexia.

A review of the literature on anorexia nervosa is frustrating, as although it is extensive, it does not in the end clarify how women come to move along the continuum of so-called normality towards the anorexic pole. What does become apparent is an ideology of femininity which is a function of the dominant gender order. This presents women with an ideal of femininity that is inherently contradictory. In the medical discourse, the voice of the object of the discourse, namely the anorexic, is never heard. Instead, she is always described, in the third person, by the spectator or observer.

Feminist theory on anorexia nervosa and feminist psychoanalytic theory give rise to a greater sense of optimism about treatment for women who self-starve. Crisp (1980), Mitchell (1980) and Bruch (1973) have used art in their otherwise traditional treatment of women diagnosed as anorexic. Art can provide an avenue for expression of aspects of the self that are difficult to verbalise. Women can also use painting and artwork in a non-hierarchical, subversive manner to explore the diverse realities common to all women in a patriarchy.

For Anne, a woman being treated for anorexia, 'Food changes the experience of where I'm at NOW . . . I'm learning other ways of getting beyond it—prayer and writing. When I'm writing, I have no eating problem' (Woodman, 1980:78). Writing and journal-keeping can be a way for women to move away from denial about their situation and release some of their intense and hurtful feelings in a manner that is safe for them. They then choose when to speak and what to share with others.

One of Kim Chernin's strategies is to ask women to close their eyes and remember the kitchen in the house where they lived as a child. I have found that writing this memory down is also a powerful way for some women to uncover their attitudes and feelings about food and diet. A diversity of experience unfolds for women and their sense of aloneness can diminish, especially when such exercises are shared with another person, whether friend, therapist or self-help group. This is a way of minimising the stigma of seeking help and of building commonality. Feminist theory and medical discourse on anorexia are both complex and creative attempts to understand the behaviour of women who self-starve. It is clear that both feminist and medical writers are motivated by compassion and a desire to help the woman diagnosed as anorexic.

Nevertheless, they do not provide consistent evidence of improved outcomes for women so labelled.

Mapping femininity

As I have suggested earlier, it is possible, drawing upon feminist and French feminist post-structuralist theory as it reinterprets Lacan, to consider the unconscious as the mediating function of self. This places the self-starver at the extreme of a continuum of values and beliefs which construct each woman's individual identity in the context of food. At another point on the continuum, the social horror and ridicule of fat women in Western culture is out of proportion to their numbers in the population and their political or social influence. Attitudes to fat women can, however, be understood in relation to the unconscious, which perhaps harbours the connection fat = out of control, or fat = someone who gives in to pleasure.

In Western society, food signifies success and failure; temptation and restraint; force and freedom; and observations about what can be called 'the other and eating'. The other, in the Lacanian sense, comprises factors outside of the subject (in this instance the eater) which, brought together, constitute meaning. For the eater, the other is the site where so-called truths about food and eating reside; the eater refers to the other in order to speak about diet and food. Individuals unconsciously know which ways of eating are appropriate to and acceptable for their gender. For women, 'feminine' ways of eating signify restraint. In the medical and lay discourse that equates femininity with restraint, those who restrain themselves too much (anorexics) and those who supposedly exhibit little restraint (fat people), become the objects of admiration or disgust; these reactions in turn enable the eater to form meaning and identity in relation to food.

For the eater in Western society, what is excluded also creates meaning. Both the anorexic and the fat woman present to the so-called normal eater unconscious images which conflict with culturally deemed appropriate behaviours towards food and diet. Food is invested with conflicting meanings, such as maintaining self-control and enjoying the good life.

Anorexia nervosa as a construct of medical and lay knowledge is part of the meal of Western logocentric philosophy and ideology which is served to the individual woman who self-starves and who tries at the same time to experience a sense of her self. It is through the acquisition of language that the individual develops a sense of self and enters the patriarchal symbolic order. This has been overlooked in the analysis of self-starving women. If the self-starving woman thinks about her embodiment in a language which is silent to the voice of a feminine plurality and autonomy, then the likelihood of her rethinking her embodiment is minimal.

Female individuation in Western culture offers women few forms that value difference in subjectivity. The woman who is treated for anorexia nervosa is lost in the jungle of dominant male definitions about embodiment that comprises lay and medical discourse. The language through which the self-starving woman articulates her experience of embodiment is, I suggest, part of an unconscious code which makes women the objects of its gaze.

To the extent that subjectivity mirrors patriarchal power relations and inscribes women's bodies in the symbolic order, it conceals the possibilities for change, for something different. 'The silence and silencing of women . . . these several centuries of silencing of women are a palpable presence in our lives—the silence we have inherited has become part of us' (Griffin, 1981:201). As Susan Griffin observes, women's reality is without a language; it is silent. In Western philosophy and scientific knowledge there is no incentive to—in Cixous's metaphor —look at the Medusa of female ways of knowing. Roland Barthes's elaboration of the real without language is relevant here:

Thus at this moment I am not describing any 'authentic' experience, giving the picture of any 'real' teaching, opening any 'university' dossier. For writing can tell the truth on language but not the truth on the real [we are at present trying to find out what a real without language is]. (Barthes, 1971:203)

This production of meaning and identity is articulated through a language which privileges masculine forms of cognition and hides the imaginary or symbolic and which is without language. The language of the subject 'I' is a male language which presupposes women as the objects of its gaze. The woman who self-starves conceives of her self as that which the anorexia creates; non-anorexic aspects of her self become the other. The label 'anorexic' leads women to interpret their experiences, behaviour and feelings in terms of the language of that diagnostic category. Aspects of self which are not included in the definition of how a 'typical' anorexic behaves are obscured in the treatment process. It is difficult for a woman to have an experience as the subject of the discourse which is not inherently defined by the masculine. The self-starver may be diminishing her sense of the non-anorexic woman-self who has desire and jouissance. The self-starving woman is, like all women, in a discourse in which femininity is constructed by male meanings in a patriarchy, and which therefore avoids female ways of expression, corporeality and the feminine imaginary.

Women may seek different places in the medical and lay discourse about diet, where a fluid sense of femininity can emerge and challenge established codes of meaning as they relate to eating, food and embodiment. By locating the lacunas in the lay and medical discourse, women may create meanings in the space (difference) between words, rather than in the words themselves. The self-starver, via a non-relational, hitherto marginalised path of conceptualisation and expression, may find her own sense of corporeality.

For women, this will be an exploratory journey in

search of the gaps, under-meanings and un-meanings. It may be similar to Deleuze and Guattari's journey into concepts of non-directional, non-territorial drives which interrupt the surface tension of the self. I do not intend to make an exegesis of their work (I suggest a reading of *Anti-Oedipus* (Deleuze & Guattari, 1977)). What is relevant to a discussion of self-starvation is their attempt to free desire from goals and to encourage new forms in language. The physical body, they assert, must be protected from the old codes: 'Psychoanalysis should not be content with designating cases, analyzing personal histories, or diagnosing complexes. As a psychoanalysis of meaning, it should be geographic before being anecdotal: it should distinguish between different regions' (Deleuze, 1979:294). Understanding for the self-starving woman could include an examination of under-meanings—a geography of forms of meaning which includes space for the codes of jouissance and at the same time deconstructs femininity and subjectivity. As Irigaray has said, this is possible in the process of drawing out the connections between psychic phenomena and linguistic discursive constructions (Irigaray, 1974).

This process is fraught with complexities. I am well aware of the difficulty of attempting to establish geographic forms of meaning in treatment, even with the aim of encouraging an empowering sense of embodiment for the self-starving woman. Geographic meanings are to be found in a movement between the accepted codes of embodiment in the dominant discourse. Here the spaces and silences in the discourse can be the source for a fluid, non-hierarchicalised femininity. In the subtle power relationship found in all forms of therapy, feminist or traditional, it is difficult, yet possible, to find such geographic meanings. The question is whether it is possible to subvert the discourse which constructs femininity for women in an oppressive manner without at the same time becoming part of a unitary conceptualisation of the self-starving woman, or anorexic, and thereby objectifying women who self-starve into a reverse discourse.

I do not have definitive answers. Nor do I believe that there is a single answer to problems with eating and dieting. Yet paradoxically therapy, while not the solution, may be part of a process which leads women to an understanding of the social factors that contribute to their problem. Of the construction of femininity in twentieth-century Australia, Jill Mathews observes: 'The realisation of the historical construction of our individual sense of failure can open up new possibilities that we are not afraid to try' (Mathews, 1984:201). An understanding of the historical position of women and the way in which femininity is constructed can contribute to recovery from anorexia. Traditional treatment participates in silencing women at a time when they most need to discover for themselves a vocabulary of words and non-verbal ways in which to express thoughts and feelings about their lives. This may involve physically acting or re-enacting situations and themes that they have found problematic.

In my experience, creating a space where women can speak about their understanding of food and their concerns in relation to it provides a way of cutting across the male discourse. Women coming for feminist therapy want their emotional pain to stop, and seek out places that may help them. They are usually looking for an alternative to traditional practice, and they come of their own accord. A person working alongside a woman with eating problems can help to draw out the anorexic text within her, an internalised text of illness behaviour. Thinking and speaking about the meaning of this anorexic text may lead to a territory where the self-starving woman can nourish herself and develop the skills to become independent and empowered. I have seen some women discover their own maps to recovery from their eating problems. This process is itself a mapping of the social construction of anorexia.

There is a distinction between feminist therapists who try to establish alternative treatments for the constructed entity 'the anorexic', and feminists who work alongside self-starving women in deconstructing the totalised object —the anorexic. Journeying alongside the woman who is seeking help involves not an interpretation of how her behaviour, emotions and psyche fit her into a category labelled 'anorexic', but rather an expression of the diverse realities she experiences. It is possible to articulate other parts of the self outside of so-called typical anorexic patterns. At the same time, the lost choices and options that women relinquish in assuming such labels as 'anorexic' can be expressed.

This approach suggests strategies for recovery in the face of the pervasive knowledges that would crush women into shape. Feminist therapists, moreover, continually run the risk of co-option. We do not work in isolation, and at times it is difficult to avoid falling into male-stream therapy, especially when the starvation is life-threatening. Weight restoration to save a woman's life and stabilise her nutritionally is a first priority in such instances. Yet it is vital that in the process the woman with the weight-loss symptoms is not obscured, and that an anorexic identity is not created for her.

As Fiona Place writes, 'The battle to find words to express the world as it is—full of paradoxes and not the narrow simple place some parents describe it to be—often leaves the person with anorexia feeling confused and isolated' (Place, 1989:268). An understanding of the elements of her experience that derive from her position as a woman in our society creates an opportunity to re-make sense of these experiences as one of the many ways to recovery. This is a process of discovery of the maps of femininity in society and of the creation of a space for the expression of the paradoxes, slips and confusion that all women, not only those labelled anorexic, experience. In writing and drawing about these metaphorical maps, women are able to speak about some of their experiences in a different context.

Lest their experience be passed over in silence, it is vital that self-starving women be encouraged to write, speak and be heard. Some women find it useful to write their own versions of their case histories in the form of bogus dossiers on the treatment they have received for their eating problems. By switching from the third person to the first person, women can experience the ways in which the subject is located within the various discourses about anorexia. For example, one woman wrote 'anorexics mostly are difficult, phobic and hard to treat', as opposed to 'I was told I was mostly difficult, phobic and hard to treat'. I prefer to think of this process as double-dealing the prevailing discourse.

The person working with the woman with eating problems avoids the construction of 'the anorexic patient' by resisting the impulse to label her behaviour clinically. Once a woman assumes the clinical identity of an anorexic it is difficult for her to see the non-anorexic parts of herself. Working with the woman who self-starves involves encouraging her to speak through, around, underneath and above the maze of symptoms she experiences, without at the same time moulding her into a clinical category.

The laughter that emerges from this mapping of the lacuna in the clinical discourse is absent from most writing about anorexia. Laughter and pleasure are milestones to recovery which appear in discussions with women about the hiatus between what society tells us is pleasure and desire, and how we actually experience it. Playfulness, games and music are some of the ways that women can involve their whole bodies in recovery. It is extraordinary how even a little pleasure and laughter marks progress across the map and signals that the starving is coming to an end.

Given the emptiness, loneliness and suffering of women seeking help, it is crucial, in mapping femininity and recovery with women, to create a space for difference. Recovery is possible, but not through the adoption of clinical labels. The friend, counsellor or peer needs to avoid all strategies that would limit the self-starving woman's definition of herself in her own words, her own language and her own voice. I hope this book will help to open some spaces for alternative views and a deconstruction of the text of self-starvation. And I hope women who have experienced self-starvation will find the courage and strength to write and speak about their experience and about their ways of knowing in the margins of the discourse. In doing so, they may find pathways to places in which delight in a variety of sizes, shapes and voices of women expresses the differences, contrasts and jouissance of a plurality of femininity.

Bibliography

Abraham, S. and Llewellyn-Jones, D. 1984, *Eating Disorders: The Facts*, Oxford University Press, Sydney

Agras, W.S. and Kramer, H.C. 1984, 'The treatment of anorexia nervosa: Do different treatments have different outcomes' *Eating and Its Disorders*, eds A.J. Stunkard and E. Stellar, Raven Press, New York

Andre-Thomas, C. 1909, 'Anorexic mentale', *La Clinique*, vol. 4, p. 33

Ardener, S. (ed) 1981, *Women and Space: Ground Rules and Social Maps*, Croom Helm, London

Armstrong, D. 1982, 'The doctor–patient relationship 1930–80', *The Problem of Medical Knowledge*, eds P. Wright and A. Treacher Edinburgh University Press, Edinburgh

Atkinson, P. 1984, 'Eating virtue', *The Sociology of Food and Eating*, ed A. Murcott, Gower, Aldershot, UK

Australian Government Commission of Inquiry into Poverty 1976, Australian Government Publishing Service, Canberra

Baldock, C.V. 1983, 'Public policies and the paid work of women' *Women, Social Welfare and the State in Australia*, C.V. Baldock and B. Cass, Allen and Unwin, Sydney

Barthes, R. 1973, 'Wine and milk' *Mythologies*, R. Barthes, Paladin Books, London

—— 1971, 'Ecrivains, intellectuals, professeurs', *Image, Music, Text*, ed S. Heath (1984) Fontana, London

Bell, R.M. 1985, *Holy Anorexia*, University of Chicago Press, Chicago

Bem, S.L. 1974, 'The measurement of psychological androgyny', *Journal of Consulting and Clinical Psychology*, 42, pp. 155–62

Bemis, K.M. 1978, 'Current approaches to the aetiology and treatment of anorexia nervosa', *Psychological Bulletin*, 85, pp. 593–617

Benveniste, E. 1971, *Problems in General Linguistics*, University of Miami Press, Miami.

Berndt, C. 1978, 'Digging sticks and spears, or the two-sex model', *Women's Role in Aboriginal Society*, ed F. Gale, Australian Institute of Aboriginal Studies, Canberra

Berg, E.L. 1982, 'The third woman', *Diacritics* Summer

Binswaanger, L. 1944, 'Der Fall Ellen West' *Existence*, eds R. May, E. Angel and H. Ellenberger (1958), Basic Books, New York

Black, C. (ed) 1915 (reprinted 1983), *Married Women's Work* Virago, London

Blaxter, M. and Paterson, E. 1984, 'The goodness is out of it: The meaning of food to two generations', *The Sociology of Food and Eating*, A. Murcott, Gower, Aldershot, UK

Bliss, E.L. and Branch, C.H. 1960, *Anorexia Nervosa: Its History, Psychology and Biology*, Paul B. Hoeber, New York

Bolton, J. 1972, 'Food taboos among the Orang Asli in west Malaysia: A potential nutritional hazard', *American Journal of Clinical Nutrition*, 25, pp. 789–99

Bordo, S. 1988, 'Anorexia nervosa: Psychopathology as crystallization of culture' *Feminism and Foucault*, I. Diamond and L. Quinby, Northeastern University Press, Boston

Boskind-White, M. 1979, 'Cinderella's stepsisters: A feminist perspective on anorexia nervosa and bulimia', *Psychology of Women*, ed J.H. Williams, W.W. Norton, New York

Breuer, J. 1890, 'Studies on hysteria by Josef Breuer and Sigmund Freud', *The Complete Psychological Works of Sigmund Freud* (standard edition, ed J. Strachey (1956)), vol. VII, Hogarth Press, London

Bromley, E. 1983, 'Anorexia nervosa: Counselling and self-help groups—an introduction', *Current Issues in Clinical Psychology, Vol. 1*, ed E. Karas, Plenum Press, New York

Broverman, I.K., Broverman, D.M., et al. 1970, 'Sex role stereotypes and clinical judgments of mental health', *Journal of Consulting and Clinical Psychology*, vol. 34, no. 1, pp. 1–7

Bruch, H. 1962, 'Perceptual and conceptual disturbances in anorexia nervosa', *Psychosomatic Medicine* 24, pp. 188–194

—— 1973, *Eating Disorders: Obesity, Anorexia Nervosa and the Person Within*, Routledge and Kegan Paul, London

—— 1976, *The Golden Cage: The Enigma of Anorexia Nervosa*, Routledge and Kegan Paul, London

Brumberg, J.J. 1982, 'Chlorotic girls, 1870–1920: A historical perspective on female adolescence', *Women and Health in America: Historical Readings*, J.W. Leavitt, University of Wisconsin Press, Madison, Wisconsin

Busfield, J. 1983, 'Gender, mental illness and psychiatry' *Sexual Divisions*, M. Evans and C. Ungerson, Tavistock Publications, London

Charcot, J.M. 1885, 'De l'isolement dans le traitement de l'hysterie', *Progr. med.*, Paris, 1, p. 161

Chernin, K. 1986, *The Hungry Self: Women, Eating and Identity*, Virago, London

Chidio, J. and Latimer, P.R. 1983, 'Vomiting as a learned weight-control technique in bulimia', *Journal of Behavioural Therapy and Experimental Psychiatry* 14, p. 131

Chodorow, N. 1978, *The Reproduction of Mothering*, University of California Press, Berkeley

Cixous, H. 1976, 'The laugh of the Medusa' *Signs*, vol. 1, no. 4, p. 885

—— 1981, 'Castration or decapitation?' *Signs*, Autumn

Cleo 1987, 'Is a food obsession ruining your life?' September, p. 97

Comaroff, J. 1982, 'Medicine: Symbol and ideology', *The Problem of Medical Knowledge*, eds P. Wright and A. Treacher Edinburgh University Press, Edinburgh

Cosmopolitan 1988, 'Starving for attention', November, p. 164

Constantine, S. 1987, 'The weaker sex: Food and feminism', *Arena* 79, p. 119

Crawford, D. and Worsley, A. 1988, 'Dieting and slimming practices of South Australian women', *Medical Journal of Australia* 148, pp. 325–31

Crisp, A.H., Palmer, R.L., and Kalucy, R.S. 1976, 'How common is anorexia nervosa? A prevalence study', *British Journal of Psychiatry* 128, pp. 549–554

Crisp, A.H., Kalucy, R.S., and Palmer, R.L. 1983, 'Body experience and adolescence in the female', *The Young Woman: Psychosomatic Aspects of Obstetrics and Gynaecology*, eds L. Dennerstein and M. De Saunders Excerpta Medica, Dublin

Crisp, A.H. 1980, *Anorexia Nervosa: Let Me Be*, Academic, London

Davis, A. and George, J. 1988, *States of Health: Health and Illness in Australia*, Harper and Row, Sydney

De Beauvoir, S. 1949, *The Second Sex* (trans. 1974), Jonathan Cape, London

Deleuze, G. and Guattari, F. 1972, 'L'anti-Oedipe' *Anti-Oedipus, Capitalism and Schizophrenia* (1977) Viking, New York

Deleuze, G. 1979, 'The schizophrenic and language: Surface and depth in Lewis Carroll and Antonin Artaud', *Textual Strategies: Perspectives in Post-Structuralist Criticism*, J.V. Harari, Cornell University Press, Ithaca, New York

Dennerstein, L. and Senarclens, M. (eds) 1983, 'The young woman: Psychosomatic aspects of obstetrics and gynaecology', *7th International Congress of Psychosomatic Obstetrics and Gynaecology*, Excerpta Medica, Dublin

Derrida, J. 1967, 'L'Ecriture et la différence', *Writing and Difference* (1978), University of Chicago Press, Chicago

Derrida, J. and McDonald, C.V. 1982, 'Interview: Choreographies', *Diacritics*, vol. 12, p. 12

De Saussure, F. 1966, *Course in General Linguistics*, McGraw-Hill, New York

Diagnostic and Statistical Manual of Mental Disorders, 1980, 3rd edn, American Psychiatric Association

Donnison, J. 1977, *Midwives and Medical Men*, Heinemann, London

Donovan, J. 1985, *Feminist Theory*, Frederick Ungar, New York

Douglas, M. (ed) 1984, 'Standard social usages of food', *Food and the Social Order: Studies of Food and Festivities in Three American Communities*, Russell Sage Foundation, New York

Driver, C. 1983, *The British at Table, 1940–1980*, Chatto and Windus, London

Duddle, M. 1973, 'An increase of anorexia nervosa in a university population', *British Journal of Psychiatry* 123, pp. 711–712

Douglas, M. and Isherwood, B. 1979, *The World of Goods: Towards an Anthropology of Consumption*, Allen Lane, London

Dwyer, J.T. 1982, 'Vegetarian, health and junk foods' *Manual of clinical nutrition*, ed D. Paige Nutrition Publications, Pleasantville, N.J.

Edwards, G. 1983, 'Counselling for clients with anorexia nervosa', *Current Issues in Clinical Psychology, Vol. 1*, ed E. Karas, Plenum Press, New York

Ehrenreich, B. and English, D. 1973, *Complaints and Disorders: The Sexual Politics of Sickness*, Feminist Press, Old Westbury, New York

Elias, N. 1978, *The Civilizing Process: The History of Manners*, Urizen Books, New York

Emmett, S.W. 1985, *Theory and Research of Anorexia and Bulimia*, Bruner Mazel, New York

Engels, F. 1958, *The Condition of the Working Classes in England in 1844* (reprint of 1845 edition) Stanford University Press, Stanford, California

Evans, J. et al. (eds) 1986, *Feminism and Political Theory*, Sage Publications, London

Fallon, A.E. and Rozin, P. 1983, 'The psychological bases of food rejections by humans', *Ecology of Food and Nutrition*, no. 13, pp. 15–26

Farb, P. and Armelagos, G. 1980, *Consuming Passions*, Houghton Mifflin, Boston

Feighner, J.P. (ed) 1972, 'Diagnostic criteria for use in psychiatric research', *Archives of General Psychiatry*, 26, pp. 57–63

Figlio, K. 1978, 'Chlorosis and chronic diseases in 19th century Britain: The social constitution of somatic illness in a capitalist society', *International Journal of the Health Sciences*, no. 8, pp. 589–616

—— 1976, 'The metaphor of organisation: A historiographical perspective on the biomedical sciences of the early nineteenth century', *History of Science*, no. 14, pp: 17–55

Foucault, M. 1971, *Madness and Civilisation: A History of Insanity in the Age of Reason*, Vintage, New York
—— 1973, *Birth of the Clinic: An Archaeology of Medical Perception*, Tavistock, London
—— 1977, *Discipline and Punish: The Birth of the Prison*, Allen Lane, London
—— 1978, *The History of Sexuality, Vol. 1: An Introduction*, Allen Lane, London
—— 1979, 'What is an Author?', *Textual Strategies: Perspectives in Post-Structuralist Criticism*, J.V. Harari, Cornell University Press, Ithaca, New York
—— 1980, *Power and Knowledge: Selected Interviews and Other Writings, 1972–1977*, ed C. Gordon et al., Pantheon Books, New York
—— 1982, 'The Subject & Power' *M. Foucault: Beyond Structuralism & Hermeneutics*, eds H. Dreyfus & P. Rabinow, University of Chicago Press, Chicago
Freidson, E. 1975, *Profession of Medicine: A Study of the Sociology of Medical Knowledge*, Dodd Mead, New York
Freud, A. 1958, 'Adolescence', *Psychoanalytic Study of the Child* no. 13, pp. 225–287
Freud, S. 1953, 'Mourning and Melancholia', *The Complete Psychological Works of Sigmund Freud* (standard edition, ed J. Strachey (1956)), vol. XIV, pp. 243–58, Hogarth Press, London
Friesh, H. 1977, 'Studies on secondary amenorrhea, anorectic behaviour, and body-image perception: Importance for the early recognition of anorexia nervosa', *Anorexia Nervosa*, ed R.A. Vigersky, Raven Press, New York
Gabbay, J. 1982, 'Asthma attacked? Tactics for the reconstruction of a disease concept', *The Problem of Medical Knowledge*, eds P. Wright and A. Treacher, Edinburgh University Press, Edinburgh
Gamarnikow, E., Morgan, D., et al. (eds) 1983, *The Public and the Private*, Heinemann, London
Ganner, D.M. and Garfinkel, P.E. 1978, 'Sociocultural factors in anorexia nervosa', *The Lancet*, September 2, p. 674
Garfinkel, P.E. and Garner, D. 1982, *Anorexia Nervosa: A Multidimensional Perspective*, Brunner Mazel, New York
Garner, D.M., Garfinkel, P.E., et al. 1976, 'Body image disturbance in anorexia nervosa and obesity', *Psychosomatic Medicine* no. 38, pp. 227–237
George, J. 1986, 'Women, health policy and social work: Dilemmas of theory and practice', *Gender Reclaimed: Women in Social Work*, eds H. Marchant and B. Wearing, Hale and Iremonger, Sydney
Giorgi, A. (ed) 1985, *Phenomenology and Psychological Research*, Duquesne University Press, Pittsburg
Goody, J. 1982, *Cooking, Cuisine and Class*, Cambridge University Press, Cambridge

Gordon, C. (ed) 1986, *Michel Foucault: Power/Knowledge*, Harvester, Bristol

Gove, W.R., and Tudor, J.F. 1972, 'Adult sex roles and mental illness', *American Journal of Sociology* 78, pp. 812–35

Griffin, S. 1981, *Pornography and Silence*, Harper and Row, London

Grosz, E.A. (1990) *Jacques Lacan: A feminist introduction*, Routledge, London, New York

Gull, W.W. 1868, 'The address in medicine', *Evolution of Psychosomatic Concepts: Anorexia Nervosa, a Paradigm*, eds M.R. Kaufman and M. Heiman (1964) International Universities Press, New York

Hahn, R.A., 'Culture-bound syndromes unbound', *Social Science and Medicine*, vol. 21, no. 2, pp. 165–171

Hall, D. 1976, *The Natural Health Book*, Thomas Nelson, Melbourne

Hand, W.D. and Stevenson, L.G. 1980, *Magical Medicine*, University of California Press, Berkeley

Harari, J.V. 1979, *Textual Strategies: Perspectives in Post-Structuralist Criticism*, Cornell University Press, Ithaca, New York

Harding, S. and Hintikka, M.B. (eds) 1983, *Discovering Reality*, D. Reidel, Dordrecht, Holland

Harris, L.J. 1981, 'Sex-related variations in spatial skill', *Spatial Representation and Behaviour Across the Lifespan*, eds L.S. Liben et al. Academic Press, New York

Harris, M. 1979, *Cultural Materialism*, Random House, New York

Harris, M. and Ross, E.B. 1987, *Food and Evolution*, Temple University Press, Philadelphia

Hartley, P.M. 1983, 'The value of self-help groups in anorexia nervosa', *Current Issues in Clinical Psychology, Vol. 1*, ed E. Karas, Plenum Press, New York

Hawkes, T. 1977, *Structuralism and Semiotics*, Methuen, London

Hecht, J.A. 1985, 'Physical and social Pukapukan theories of disease', *Healing Practices in the South Pacific*, C. Parsons, Institute of Polynesian Studies, University of Hawaii Press, Laie, Hawaii

Hiatt, L.R. 1965, *Kinship and Conflict: A Study of an Aboriginal Community in northern Arnhem Land*, Australian National University Press, Canberra

Hueneman, R.L., Shapiro, L.R. et al. 1966, 'A longitudinal study of gross body composition and body conformation and their association with food and activity in a teenage population: views of teenage subjects on body conformation, food and activity', *American Journal of Clinical Nutrition*, vol. 18, pp. 325–338

Ingleby, D. 1982, 'The social construction of mental illness', *The Problem of Medical Knowledge*, eds P. Wright and A. Treacher, Edinburgh University Press, Edinburgh

Innis, R.E. 1985, *Semiotics*, Indiana University Press, Indianapolis

Irigaray, L. 1985, *Speculum of the Other Woman*, Cornell University Press, Ithaca, New York

—— 1981, 'And the one doesn't stir without the other', *Signs* vol. 7, no. 1, pp. 60–67

—— 1985, *This Sex Which is Not One*, Cornell University Press, Ithaca, New York

Janet, P. 1907, *The Major Symptoms of Hysteria*, Macmillan, London

Jaspers, K. 1963, *General Psychopathology*, University of Chicago Press, Chicago

Jordanova, L.J. 1980, 'Natural facts: A historical perspective on science and sexuality', *Nature, Culture and Gender*, eds C. MacCormack and M. Strathan, Cambridge University Press, Cambridge

—— 1982, 'Conceptualizing power over women', *Radical Science Journal*, no. 12, pp. 124–128

Karas, E. (ed) 1983, *Current Issues in Clinical Psychology, Vol. 1*, Plenum Press, New York

Katona-Apte, J. 1975, 'The relevance of nourishment to the reproductive cycle of the female in India' *Being Female and Reproduction, Power and Change*, ed D. Raphael Mouton, The Hague

Kelly, A. 1981, *The Missing Half*, Manchester University Press, Manchester

Kessler, S. and McKenna, W. 1982, 'Developmental aspects of gender', *The Changing Experience of Women*, eds E. Whitelegg, M. Arnot, E. Bartels et al. The Open University, Martin Robertson and Co, Oxford

Khare, R.S. and Rao, M.S.A. (eds) 1986, *Food, Society and Culture*, Carolina Academic Press, Durham, North Carolina

Kinoy, B.P. (ed) 1984, *When Will We Laugh Again? Living and Dealing with Anorexia Nervosa and Bulimia*, Columbia University Press, New York

Kuhn, R. 1953, Zur Daseinsanalyse der anorexia mentalis. II. *Studie. Nervenarzt* 24, p. 191

Lacan, J. 1972, 'God and the jouissance of the woman', *Feminine Sexuality* (1982) Macmillan, London

—— 1975, *Le Seminaire 1: Les ecrits techniques de Freud*, Seuil, Paris

—— 1975, *Encore. Le seminaire Livre XX*. Seuil, Paris

—— 1977, *Ecrits. A Selection*, Tavistock, London

Lasegue, E.C. 1873, 'De l'anorexie hysterique', *Evaluation of Psychosomatic Concepts: Anorexia Nervosa, A Paradigm*, eds M.R. Kaufman and M. Heiman (1964) International Universities Press, New York

Lawrence, M. 1984, *The Anorexic Experience*, The Women's Press, London

Leavitt, J.W. 1984, *Women and Health in America: Historical Readings*, University of Wisconsin Press, Madison, Wisconsin

Lehrer, A. 1972, 'Cooking vocabularies and the culinary triangle of Levi-Strauss', *Anthropological Linguistics*, vol. 14, pp. 155–171

Lemaire, A. 1977, *Jacques Lacan*, Routledge and Kegan Paul, London

Lenon, R.A. 1985, 'Anorexia nervosa: Medical management', *Transactional Analysis Journal*, vol. 15, no. 1, January

Levi-Strauss, C. 1965, 'Le triangle culinaire', *Partisan Review*, vol. 33, pp. 586–595

Levy, R. 1976, 'Psychosomatic symptoms and women's protest: two types of reaction to structural strain in the family', *Journal of Health and Social Behaviour* 17 (June), pp. 122–34

Liddington, J. and Norris, J. 1978, *One Hand Tied Behind Us*, Virago, London

Logue, A.W. 1986, *The Psychology of Eating and Drinking*, W.H. Freeman, New York

Low, S.A., 'Culturally interpreted symptoms or CIS: A Cross-Cultural Review of Nerves', *Social Science and Medicine* vol. 21, no. 2, pp. 87–196

Maccoby, E.E. (ed) 1967, *The Development of Sex Differences*, Tavistock, London

Maccoby, E.E. and Jacklin, C.N. (eds) 1974, *The Psychology of Sex Differences*, Stanford University Press, Stanford, California

Maeroff, G.I. 1975, 'Males excel in tests', *New York Times*, October 13

MacLeod, S. 1981, *The Art of Starvation*, Virago, London

Marks, E. and Courtivron, I. 1981, *New French Feminisms*, Schocken Books, New York

Mathews, J.J. 1984, *Good and Mad Women*, George Allen and Unwin, Sydney

Mennell, S. 1987, 'On the civilizing of appetite', *Theory, Culture and Society*, Sage Publications, London, vol. 4, pp. 373–403

Messer, E. 1984, 'Anthropological perspectives on diet', *Annual Review of Anthropology* no. 13, pp. 205–49

Minuchin, P. 1964, 'Sex role concepts and sex typing in childhood as a function of school and home environments', Proceedings of American Orthopsychiatric Association Conference, Chicago

Minuchin, S., Rosman, B.L. and Baker, L. 1978, *Psychosomatic Families: Anorexia Nervosa in Context*, Harvard University Press, Cambridge, Massachusetts

Mitchell, D. 1980, 'Anorexia Nervosa', *Arts in Psychotherapy*, no. 7, pp. 53–60

Mitchell, J. 1974, *Psychoanalysis and feminism*, Penguin, Harmondsworth

Mitchell, J. and Rose, J. (eds) 1982, *Feminine sexuality: Jacques Lacan and the Ecole Freudienne*, Macmillan, London

Mitchell, J.E. (ed) 1985, *Anorexia Nervosa and Bulimia*, University of Minnesota, Minneapolis

Mitchell, S.W. 1881, *Lectures on Diseases of the Nervous System*, Henry C. Leas, Philadelphia

Moi, T. 1985, *Sexual Textual Politics*, Methuen, London

Morantz, R.M. and Zscmoche, S. 1984, 'Professionalism, feminism and gender roles: A comparative study of 19th-century medical therapeutics', *Women and Health in America: Historical Readings*, ed J.W. Leavitt, University of Wisconsin Press, Madison, Wisconsin

Morton, R. 1694, in J. Silverman (1983), 'Richard Morton, 1637–1698: Limner of Anorexia Nervosa: His Life and Times' *Journal of the American Medical Association*, 250, (Nov 25)

Mounin, G. 1985, *Semiotic Praxis*, Plenum Press, New York

Murcott, A. (ed) 1984, *The Sociology of Food and Eating*, Gower, Aldershot, UK

Muskett 1908, 'The attainment of health and the treatment of the different diseases by means of diet', quoted in *From Scarcity to Surfeit*, R. Walker and D. Roberts (1988), University of NSW Press, Sydney

Myerhoff, B. 1978, 'Bobbes and Zeydes: Old and new roles for elderly Jews', *Women in Ritual and Symbolic Roles*, J. Hock-Smith and A. Spring, Plenum Press, New York

Naudeau, 1789, 'Observation sur une maladie nerveuse accompagnée d'un dégout extraordinaire pour les alimens', *J. Med. Chir. et. Pharmacol*, 80, p. 197

New Internationalist, 1986, 'You are what you eat', no. 160, June, p. 13

Newton, J. and Rosenfelt, D. (eds) 1985, *Feminist Criticism and Social Change*, Methuen, New York

Numbers, R.L. and Schoepflin, R.B. 1984, 'Ministries of healing' (eds), *Women and Health in America*, ed J.W. Leavitt, University of Wisconsin Press, Madison

Nylander, I. 1971, 'The feeling of being fat and dieting in the school population', *Acta Sociomedica Scandinavia*, 3, pp. 17–26

Oakley, A. 1984, *The Captured Womb: A history of the medical care of pregnant women*, Blackwell, Oxford

O'Neill, J. 1985, *Five Bodies: The Human Shape of Modern Society*, Cornell University Press, Ithaca, New York

Orbach, S. 1986, *Hunger Strike: The Anorectic's Struggle as a Metaphor for our Age*, Faber and Faber, London

—— 1985, 'Visibility/invisibility: Social considerations in anorexia nervosa', *Theory and Treatment of Anorexia Nervosa*, S.W. Emmett, Bruner Mazel, New York

Ortner, S.B. 1974, 'Is female to male as nature is to culture?' *Woman, Culture and Society*, eds M. Zimbalist Rosaldo and L. Lamphere, Stanford University Press, Stanford, California

Palazzoli, M.S. 1965, 'Interpretation of mental anorexia', *Anorexia Nervosa*, eds J.E. Meyer and H. Feldman, Thieme, Stuttgart

Palazzoli, M.S. 1974, *Self-Starvation: From the Intrapsychic to the Transpersonal Approach to Anorexia Nervosa*, Human Context Books, London

Palmer, R.L. 1980, *Anorexia Nervosa*, Penguin, New York

Parsons, C.D. 1985, *Healing Practices in the South Pacific*, Institute of Polynesian Studies, University of Hawaii Press, Laie, Hawaii

Pateman, C. and Grosz, E. (eds) 1986, *Feminist Challenges: Social and Political Theory*, Allen and Unwin, Sydney

Pirke, K.M. and Ploog, D. (eds) 1984, *The Psycho-biology of Anorexia Nervosa*, Springer-Verlag, Berlin

Place, F. 1989, *Cardboard*, Local Consumption Pub, University of Sydney, Sydney

Prince, R. 1985, 'The concept of culture-bound syndromes: Anorexia nervosa and brain fag', *Soc. Sci. Med.*, vol. 21, no. 2, pp. 197–203

Pringle, R. 1983, 'Women and consumer capitalism', *Women, Social Welfare and the State in Australia*, C.V. Baldock and B. Cass, Allen and Unwin, Sydney

Rich, A. 1976, *Of Woman Born*, Bantam Books, New York

Riessman, C.K. 1983, 'Women and medicalization: A new perspective', *Social Policy*, 14, pp. 3–18

Rizvi, N. 1986, 'Food categories in Bangladesh and its relationship to food beliefs and practices of vulnerable groups', *Food, Society and Culture*, R.S. Khare and M.S.A. Rao, Carolina Academic Press, Durham, North Carolina

Roberts, E. 1984, *A Woman's Place: An Oral History of Working Class Women 1890–1940*, Blackwell, Oxford

Rose, J. 1987, 'Femininity and its discontents' *Sexuality: A Reader*, ed *Feminist Review*, Virago, London

Rozin, P. 1987, 'Psychobiological perspectives on food preferences and avoidances', *Food and Evolution*, M. Harris and E.B. Ross, Temple University Press, Philadelphia

Ruesch, J. 1972, *Semiotic Approaches to Human Relations*, Mouton, The Hague

Russell, G.F.M. 1970, 'Anorexia nervosa: Its identity as an illness and its treatment', *Modern Trends in Psychological Medicine*, ed J.H. Prince Appleton-Century-Crofts, New York

Ryle, J.A. 1936, 'Anorexia nervosa', *Lancet*, 231, pp. 892–894

Sayers, J. 1986, *Sexual Contradictions*, Tavistock, London

Schwab, J.J. and Schwab, M.E. 1978, *Sociocultural Roots of Mental Illness: An Epidemiological Study*, Plenum Press, New York

Schwartz, D.M., Thompson, M. and Johnson, C. 1982, 'Anorexia and bulimia: The sociocultural context', *International Journal of Eating Disorders*, 1, pp. 23–35

Sebeok, T.A. (ed) 1971, *Approaches to Semiotics*, Mouton, The Hague

Shack, W. 1971, 'Hunger, anxiety and ritual: Deprivation and spirit possession among the Gurage of Ethiopia', *Man* (NS) 6 (1):30–43

Shaver, P. and Hendrick, C. 1987, 'Sex and gender', *Review of*

Personality and Social Psychology, 7, Sage Publications, Beverly Hills, California

Sheehan, H.L. 1939, 'Simmonds' disease due to postpartum necrosis of anterior pituitary', *Quarterly Journal of Medicine*, 8, pp. 277–281

Shorter, E. 1982, *A History of Women's Bodies*, Allen Lane, London

Showalter, E. 1985, *The Female Malady: Women, Madness, and English Culture 1830–1980*, Pantheon Books, New York

Simmonds, M. 1914, 'Uber hypophysisschwund mit todlichem aus gang', *Deutsche Medizinische Wochenschrift* 40, pp. 332–340

Sitnick, T. and Katz, J.L. 1983, 'Sex role identity and anorexia nervosa', *International Journal of Eating Disorders*, vol. 12, p. 82

Slade, P.D. and Russell, G.F.M. 1973, 'Experimental investigations of body perceptions in anorexia nervosa and obesity', *Psychotherapy and psychosomatics*, 22, pp. 359–363

Slade, P. 1983, 'The role of counselling and self help groups in the management of anorexia nervosa', *Current Issues in Clinical Psychology Vol. 1*, ed E. Karas, Plenum Press, New York

Smith-Rosenberg, C. 1972, 'The hysterical woman: Sex roles and role conflict in 19th-century America', *Social Research*, 39

Smith, J.H. and Kerrigan, W. (eds) 1984, *Taking Chances: Derrida, Psychoanalysis and Literature*, Johns Hopkins University Press, Baltimore

Sours, J.A. 1980, *Starving to Death in a Sea of Objects: The Anorexia Nervosa Syndrome*, Jason Aronson, New York

Stage, S. 1979, *Female Complaints: Lydia Pinkham and the Business of Women's Medicine*, Norton, New York

Stendhal 1830, *Scarlet and Black* (1953 edn) Penguin, Harmondsworth

Stone, L. 1979, *The Family, Sex and Marriage in England 1500–1800*, Penguin, Harmondsworth

Suleiman, S.R. (ed) 1986, *The Female Body in Western Culture: Contemporary Perspectives*, Harvard University Press, Cambridge, Massachusetts

Swartz, L. 1985, 'Anorexia nervosa as a culture bound syndrome', *Social Science and Medicine*, 20, p. 725

—— 1987, 'Illness negotiation: The case of eating disorders', *Social Science and Medicine*, vol. 24, no. 7, pp. 613–618

Tabin, J.K. 1985, *On the Way to Self: Ego and Early Oedipal Development*, Columbia University Press, New York

Thoma, H. 1967, *Anorexia Nervosa*, International Universities Press, New York

Thompson, M.G. and Schwartz, D.M. 1983, 'Life adjustment of women with anorexia nervosa and anorexic-like behaviour', *International Journal of Eating Disorders*, Winter

Turner, B. 1985, *The Body and Society*, Blackwell, Oxford

Twigg, J. 1984, 'Vegetarianism and the meanings of meat', *The Sociology of Food and Eating*, ed A. Murcott, Gower, Aldershot, UK

Van Dereycken, W. and Meerman, R.A.N. 1984, *A Clinician's Guide to Treatment*, Walter de Gryter, Berlin

Walker, L.E. (ed) 1984, *Women and Mental Health Policy*, vol. 9 of *Women's Policy Studies*, Sage Publications

Walker, R. and Roberts, D. 1988, *From Scarcity to Surfeit*, NSW University Press, Sydney

Waller, J.V., Kaufman, M.R. and Deutsch, F. 1940, 'Anorexia nervosa: A psychosomatic entity', *Psychosomatic Medicine* 2, 3

Wardle, C. 1977, *Changing Food Habits in the UK*, Earth Resources Research, London

Welbourne, J. and Purgold, J. 1984, *The Eating Sickness: Anorexia, Bulimia and the Myth of Suicide by Slimming*, University of Bristol, The Harvester Press, Bristol

Williams, R. 1984, 'The salt of the earth: Ideas linking diet, exercise and virtue among elderly Aberdonians', *The Sociology of Food and Eating*, ed A. Murcott, Gower, Aldershot, UK

Wilson, E. 1987, 'Psychoanalysis: Psychic law and order?' *Sexuality a Reader*, ed *Feminist Review*, Virago, London

Woodman, M. 1980, *The Owl Was a Baker's Daughter*, Inner City Books, Toronto

Wright, P. and Treacher, A. (eds) 1982, *The Problem of Medical Knowledge*, Edinburgh University Press, Edinburgh

Index

Aboriginal diet, pre-colonial, 6, 10
Aboriginal women as food gatherers, 14
adolescent girls and anorexia nervosa, 29, 48
alternative treatment, 71; feminism and, xii, 76–7
amenorrhea, 26; diagnosis criteria, 36; psychosexual trauma and, 30; *see also* menstruation
American Psychiatric Association, 31, 42
anaemia, gender differences in diet and, 15; *see also* chlorosis; iron deficiency
anger, appetite and, 48
'Anna O' (Bertha Pappenheim), 31–2
anorexia nervosa, adolescent girls, 29, 48; biopolitics, 19; communicative disorder, as, 35; culturally induced, 49; death rate, 36; dependence and self, 51; dependency, defence against, as, 49–50; diagnosis criteria, 16, 35–7, language of, 56; 'discovery', 26; dominant gender order and feminist theory, 45;

endocrinology and 'Simmonds' disease, 29–30; feminist theories, xiii, 40–54; feminist therapy, xii, 76–7; folk term, as, 18–21; hysterical origin, 25–7; increasing prevalence, 38; indicators of, 35–7; Italian female saints and, 25; label, as, xiv; lay meanings, 18–21, 68–9; medical construct, 20–1; medical definitions, current, 35–9; medical discourse development and, 24–9; medical interpretations of, xiii, xiv, 33–5, 37; medical treatment, 31, 70; medicalisation of women's bodies and, 40; mental causes, 29–35; oral disorder, as, 33; organic basis for disease, 37; panhypopituitarism, 29–30; phenomenological theories of, 33–4; political implications of, 39, 45; psychoanalytic interpretations of, 30, 33, 59–62; psychodynamic theories of, 34; research